Space Clearing A–Z

How to Use Feng Shui
to Purify and Bless Your Home

Denise Linn

Hay House, Inc.
Carlsbad, California • Sydney, Australia

Copyright © 2001 by Denise Linn
Published and distributed in the United States by:
Hay House, Inc., P.O. Box 5100, Carlsbad, CA 92018-5100 • (800) 654-5126 • (800) 650-5115 (fax)

Editorial: Jill Kramer • *Cover Design:* Christy Salinas
Interior Design: Ashley Parsons • *Illustrations:* Jesse Riesch

The author of this book does not dispense medical advice or prescribe the use of any technique as a form of treatment for physical or medical problems without the advice of a physician, either directly or indirectly. The intent of the author is only to offer information of a general nature to help you in your quest for emotional and spiritual well-being. In the event you use any of the information in this book for yourself, which is your constitutional right, the author and the publisher assume no responsibility for your actions.

Library of Congress Cataloging-in-Publication Data

Linn, Denise.
    Space clearing A-Z : how to use Feng Shui to purify and bless your home / Denise Linn.
      p. cm.
    ISBN 1-56170-750-3 (hardcover)
    1. Feng shui. I. Title.

BF1779.F4 L56 2001
133.3'337--dc21   00-053970

ISBN 1-56170-750-3

04 03 02 01   4 3 2 1
1st printing, May 2001

Printed in China Through Palace Press International

Contents

Introduction

Have you ever walked into an empty room and immediately sensed that the atmosphere was laced with tension? You may have had no idea what occurred there prior to your arrival, yet you somehow knew that it was something unpleasant. By contrast, another place you entered gave you a feeling of joy and well-being for no apparent reason. The differences between rooms that feel great and ones that seem depressing can be explained, at least in part, by the fact that some environments are simply more beautiful or physically inviting than others. However, there is a deeper truth underlying these explanations, which relates to energy. Some environments exude an energy that is nurturing, while other spaces can deplete you and even cause you to feel depressed, irritated, or angry.

We all have the ability to sense energy. When we enter a space, we not only react to the style of the furnishings and various colors and textures, but we also perceive the energy surrounding us. Positive energy makes us feel good. Negative energy brings us down. Space Clearing offers a simple and highly effective way to turn the latter into the former. It can turn a depressing place into a haven of beauty, harmony, and effervescent joy.

Many people have heard of the art of Feng Shui for creating harmonious environments; however, most people haven't heard of Space Clearing, which is a mystical component of this ancient science. Results produced are dramatically deepened by Space Clearing, because a Feng Shui cure implemented without clearing the environment is like placing a beautiful bouquet of flowers into a dirty vase. The two done together can generate lasting, powerful results in your life.

This book teaches you specific techniques to cleanse the energy of your home, which in turn can produce a remarkable and positive influence on the way you feel, and have an effect on every aspect of your life.

For the past 30 years, I have practiced the art of cleansing and balancing home energy, a skill I named "Space Clearing." Some people call it "home healing," "smudging," or "home harmonizing." Whatever name is used, present-day Space Clearing techniques have their source in ancient techniques practiced throughout human history. The methods and tools have varied from one culture to another, but the intent has been the same—to create greater harmony and balance. Ancient ceremonies that brought vitality to human structures generations ago are once again being used to instill peace and equilibrium in today's homes and businesses. Many people are finding that these traditional rituals can be adapted very successfully for modern-day use.

People who may have never heard of Space Clearing before are now ringing bells, burning sage, and chanting mantras for the simple reason that their homes feel better as a result. Many businesses are hiring professional Space Clearers because they have found that doing so increases sales and productivity. Some of the largest real estate firms are now using the services of Space Clearers in order to dramatically accelerate their property sales. Land-management corporations are employing Space Clearers to perform blessings on the land before they build large suburban housing developments. It seems that an ancestral memory of an ancient practice has awakened, and found fertile soil in today's world.

The Space Clearing techniques that are reemerging have their source in the distant past. Throughout human history, there have been rituals for purifying and uplifting the energy of homes, temples, shrines, and public meeting places. Since earliest times, people have been performing these Space Clearing ceremonies for a very simple reason—they work!

Ancient healers understood the effect of an environment on an individual's health and well-being. In native cultures, the village shaman would perform special ceremonies to consecrate a new home or village lodge. If someone was ill, the shaman would chant, drum, and use smoking herbs—not only for the health of the person, but for cleansing and healing the entire environment they lived in. Although different tools were used in different cultures, the effect was the same. For example, Native Americans used drums, rattles, and burning herbs in their rituals. If a drum was used, its sonorous rhythm would penetrate the soul of the man or woman who was being treated, even as it simultaneously cleared the energy field of their home. The Chinese used gongs, chanting, and incense. In Medieval Europe, salt and prayers cleared energy; and in the Middle East, smoldering resins such as frankincense and myrrh were used to invite blessings into a home. After a clearing, the occupants of a dwelling felt healthier, happier, and more at peace.

There are remnants of these ancient ceremonies and practices that have been passed down through the generations to the present time. The Chinese still set off firecrackers to celebrate the beginning of the New Year. They believe that the loud noise breaks up the old stagnant energy and prepares the way for fresh new energy to flow in with the coming of another year. The practice of throwing salt over one's shoulder in order to avert evil is another example of an ancient practice that has survived into modern times. Salt has been recognized around the world as a powerful cleansing agent and is a vital component of many ancient ceremonies.

As the pace of modern living has accelerated, I believe that it is increasingly important for us to create oases of repose and serenity in our lives. Because Space Clearing has the power to transform the energy of our homes and offices, it can play a very important role in restoring balance and meaning in our lives. It is a practice that can be used on a regular basis whenever you want to shift the energy of your environment. Doing a thorough clearing of the energy of your home following an argument, after someone has been ill, in the wake of an unpleasant visitor, prior to moving into a new home, before bringing a new baby home, or even if you're just feeling out of sorts can really make a difference in your life. Space Clearing offers an easy and amazingly effective way to turn your home into a haven for your soul.

The Four Steps of Space Clearing

Space Clearing involves a four-step process. Each step is integrally linked to each of the others, and together, they create a kind of magic. These steps are: Preparation, Purification, Invocation, and Preservation.

1. Preparation

Getting ready for a Space Clearing involves preparing yourself and the space you plan to clear. To prepare the space, first you will want to do a thorough cleaning. It's also a good idea to get rid of some of the clutter. Doing a clearing in a space that has not first been cleaned and de-cluttered is like dressing in formal wear for a very special evening without bothering to first bathe and wash your hair. The results simply won't be the same.

Spend some time planning what type of Space Clearing you want to do, and then gather everything you will need for your ceremony. Each Space Clearing is as unique as the person doing it, and every ceremony should be individually tailored to the specific needs of each home or office. There is no one *best* Space Clearing method. Each method has its own beauty; however, there will be specific tools and techniques with which you may feel more aligned. To discover what is best for you, use your intuition, and imagine using the tools and doing the rituals described in this book. Some methods might feel very natural and right for you. Others may seem a bit far out or somehow not a good fit with your lifestyle. Your own intuition is the best guide to selecting the techniques that will produce the greatest results for you.

To prepare yourself for the clearing, take a purifying bath with salt or essential oils added to the water. After dressing in special clothes that you've set aside for your ceremony, you may also want to smudge yourself with ceremonial smoke. Engaging in these rituals prepares you physically, emotionally, and spiritually for your Space Clearing.

The most important aspect of the preparation stage is your overall intention for the clearing. Where intention goes, energy flows, so take some time to tune in to the source of your inner wisdom and ask yourself what you're hoping to achieve from your clearing. The more focused you become about what you envision, the easier it will be to turn that vision into reality, and the more powerful will be the transformation of your environment. The energy of the clearing will follow your intent. For example, if your intention is to fill your home with love, then the energy created by your Space Clearing will activate love.

The Blessing Altar

One of the most fun (and essential) parts of your Preparation process will be planning and collecting the necessary items for a Blessing Altar. The Blessing Altar is a temporary shrine set up at the beginning of the clearing near the entrance to the home, or in some other central location. It sets the tone and holds the energy for the entire ceremony, and it is a physical representation of your intention. It's also important because it helps to ground and integrate the energy that is stirred up in your home by the Space Clearing.

The Blessing Altar should be both beautiful and inspiring, and ought to include symbolic representations of the hopes and dreams of all the occupants of your home. Examples of objects for your Blessing Altar could be roses for love, rice for abundance, and a candle for inner light. Also, all of the Space Clearing tools that you use should be placed on this altar.

The Blessing Altar can be set up on a small table or shelf on which you have placed an Altar Cloth. The kind of fabric you choose for your Altar Cloth will greatly influence the way the entire altar feels, so this is an important choice. Homespun red cotton from South America will have a very earthy, grounded energy, while white embroidered silk will have a more formal energy that is attuned to celestial energies. The colors, textures, and fibers that you choose sets the basic tone for your Blessing Altar, which in turn will set the energy of your clearing.

2. *Purification*

This is the step where you will do your actual Space Clearing. Begin by sitting or standing before your Blessing Altar. Ask for guidance, and pray for your home and its occupants. This can be either a simple or an elaborate part of your ceremony. Gather the tools that you'll be using, such as a bell and a chime, and place them on a tray, called a Blessing Tray. You will carry this tray from room to room as you journey through your home performing Space Clearing.

As you enter the first room, place the tray down and look around the entire room to begin to assess the energy there. Stagnant energy will often make a room seem a bit hazy. You might want to walk around the circumference of the room with your hand extended, in order to "feel" the energy of the room. Stagnant or negative energy can cause your hand to feel heavy or uncomfortable in places where you encounter it.

Once you've assessed the energy, choose a tool, such as a bell, from your Blessing Tray, and stand at the entrance to the room. Take slow, deep breaths to center your-self. Imagine that you are grounded into the earth, and at the same time, connected to the heavens. With focused concentration, ring your bell. Listen carefully—it should sound crisp and clear. If it doesn't sound pristine, continue to ring your bell again until it sounds bright and distinct. This change in tone indicates that you've cleared the energy in that area. Continue around the circumference of the room in a clockwise manner (the direction normally used in the Northern Hemisphere), ringing the bell until you return to the place where you began. Move your bell in a figure-eight to seal the room. You can then choose another tool, such as the chime, to further refine the room's energy. Once again, circle the room, completing with a figure-eight. Continue using this procedure in each room until you've gone through your entire home.

Upon completion of your Space Clearing ceremony, you might want to clear the energy of the individuals who dwell in the home as well, as this deepens the effect of the house clearing. The body benefits from Space Clearing in the same way that build-ings do. Each of us has an aura of energy surrounding our physical selves, and these auras can become clogged by stress and by inner and outer influences. The methods and tools described in this book can be adapted to a personal clearing as well. For example, the same bell that you use to clear a room can be gently rung and then moved up and down the body as an individual stands, sits, or lies down. Any place on the body where the sound of the bell seems to stick or becomes dull requires a bit of extra sound generated next to it until the sound becomes clear.

3. *Invocation*

Complete your Space Clearing ceremony by returning to the Blessing Altar to say prayers and ask for blessings for all the occupants of your home. Your Space Clearing has broken up the stagnant energy and has cleared the negativity. Offering an invocation draws in the positive energy that is desired, and brings healing and transformation into the cleared space. A typical blessing might be:

"May the Creator within all things bring blessings and peace for all of the members of this household. May this home be filled with joy, laughter, and love. So be it."

Just as each clearing ceremony is individually tailored to the hopes and needs of the people who will be using the space, so, too, the Invocation will reflect the unique intention underlying the ceremony. If you wish to create a space filled with quiet, meditative energy, then your prayers will call in this kind of energy. If you want to fill your home with love and healing, ask for this to be so. Or you may wish to call in a feeling of joy and sociability. Whatever energy you invite will be the energy that permeates your home. *Ask and you shall receive.*

4. *Preservation*

The final step in Space Clearing is to preserve the new and radiant energy that you've called into the home. Doing so keeps it alive. Just as plants and other living things need to be carefully tended in order to thrive, energy also needs to be renewed in order for it to maintain its healing power. There are several ways you can preserve the energy created by Space Clearing. One way is to dedicate a small home fountain to inner peace and serenity. Thus, as the water circulates through the fountain, the intention of peace is radiating throughout your home.

Another preservation method is to place a small stone near the base of a healthy plant. Write a powerful word, wish, or symbol on the stone in waterproof ink. Or, you can paint or write your prayers on a piece of paper, which is buried in the soil of the plant. Each time the plant is watered, the words or symbol will be energized.

Setting up a permanent home altar is another wonderful method for Preservation. As you spend time meditating at your altar, your thoughts and intentions will once again connect you to the energy of your home and revitalize its power. Your home then becomes a sanctuary that is filled with love, joy, and sacred space.

❧ ❧ ❧

The A–Z List

A

Altar

A permanent home altar can generate energy that can keep an entire home balanced and clear. In ancient times, almost every home had an altar. It was traditionally placed by the hearth, or the heart, of the home and was the place where the family communed with the Divine. The home altar represented a connection between Heaven and Earth, and was a place for supplication, quiet reflection, and meditation.

There is great value in recreating this ancient tradition. An altar doesn't need to be religious. It can be a highly personal representation of what is most important to you—your hopes and dreams, joys and sorrows, and your connections to other people and to what you hold sacred. It can be a place to still your thoughts and open your heart to your own intuition. An altar can be a small haven of beauty and solace where you can retreat whenever life gets too hectic.

It's easy to make an altar. All you need is a table or shelf a bit out of the way. Spread a small, beautiful cloth on the surface, and collect things that represent your aspirations and your sense of the Creator. Although you may want to position your home shrine by the hearth, it can be placed anywhere that feels right to you. You can dedicate your altar to a special time in your life, such as a holiday or birthday; or to something you desire, such as a new job or relationship. Altars can also have themes, such as love, peace, acceptance, creativity, or abundance. However you choose to set up your altar, it should only include objects or pictures that are true representations of what is in your heart. Also, every altar ought to have a centerpoint. This can be a candle, a photo, or some other object that represents a Higher Power for you. For one person, this might be a spiritual teacher; for someone else, it might be a scene from nature. Whatever you choose for your altar's centerpoint should be something that lifts your heart every time you look at it.

The most effective altars are kept cleansed and dusted. Flowers should be fresh. Water should be replenished daily. By cleansing and purifying your home shrine, you create a template of life-force energy that permeates your entire home.

Angels

Whenever you do a Space Clearing, it's wise to ask for guidance from the realm of the angels. In every culture, there are traditions for invoking assistance from the unseen. The power that is generated by doing so can make the difference between feeling ordinary changes or experiencing small miracles resulting from your clearing. When you ask for help from angels, you are connecting to an infinite and gentle power source that can help you accomplish things you may never have imagined. The angels are around us all the time, just waiting for us to reach out to them and ask them to help us. When we do, they offer guidance, assistance, and abundant love.

Angels and fairies are attuned to the vibration of the flower kingdom. One way to invite the blessings of angels into your home during your Space Clearing is to place flower offerings in each of the rooms that you've cleared. A small saucer covered with flowers not only brings a freshness into each space, but also calls forth the devas of the angelic world. The sublime scent of essential oils made from flowers can produce the same result. The subtle smell of essential oils in an oil burner softly infusing the smell of roses or jasmine into a room can be a call to the devic kingdoms during your home clearing and blessing.

Antiques

Although antiques can add depth and beauty to a home environment, they can also embody disturbing predecessor energy, which can negatively affect the energy within your home. Predecessor energy is residual energy that the piece has accumulated from those who have owned it, and from the environments and experiences that have surrounded it during its long life. Since it's often difficult to know just what kind of energy is associated with an antique, it's a good idea to do a simple clearing for any antique that you bring into your home.

A tuning fork is the best tool to use for wooden antiques, since the penetrating quality of the fork's vibrations travels deeply into the grain of the wood. Strike the tuning fork, and then hold its base against the wood. Visualize the sound vibrations freeing any stagnant energy and releasing it, so that positive energy can flow into the piece of furniture and balance it. Antiques can also be cleared with sage or cedar smoke, or with the smoke of incense. If you have an antique that won't be damaged by the sun, placing it in sunlight for at least five hours will help purify its energy.

Aura Cleansing

A subtle energy field called an *aura* surrounds each person. Some psychics and mediums can see the colors and shape of an aura, but most people simply *feel* or *sense* a person's aura, which is a reflection of their emotions, thoughts, and state of health. A person in good health will be surrounded by a bright and clear aura; whereas someone in a negative, unhappy, or unhealthy state will be surrounded by an aura that is dull and close to the body.

The same Space Clearing techniques that you use in your home or office can be used to purify your own aura or that of another person. For example, if you use a singing bowl to cleanse your home, at the completion of your clearing ceremony, you can gently move the same singing bowl over the surface of your body and the bodies of the other members of your household. The sounds created by the bowl will penetrate the energy field of each person to brighten and lighten their aura. Within a short while, everyone should experience a positive difference in the way they feel.

Baths

After you've completed a Space Clearing, it's wise to cleanse your aura and renew your energy by taking a cleansing bath. This is also valuable for all household members to do after the clearing. Salt baths are best because of the purifying nature of salt. Dissolve a pound of salt in hot bathwater, or use Epsom salts, and soak for at least 30 minutes. You can also use aromatherapy oils in your bath. Eucalyptus is particularly powerful for cleansing, but you should dilute it in a bit of milk so that it's not too caustic to your skin. Rosemary is also beneficial. Taking a cleansing bath with salt or aromatherapy is also excellent anytime you need to prepare yourself for performing a personal cleansing, or for giving yourself a fresh new surge of energy. If you don't have a bathtub, then vigorously rub salt over your moist body, and rinse with a cold shower. This will leave your aura sparkling and bright.

Beds

We spend more time in bed than in any other place in the home. As such, the energy of the bed is very important. Ideally, you should sleep on a new mattress rather than on a secondhand one, because old mattresses can contain residual energy from previous owners. If you *do* own a used mattress, it is vital that you cleanse its energy. This can be done by placing it in sunlight, taking care to turn it so that each side is exposed to the light. If this is not possible, another effective method to use is smudging. You can use smoking sage to completely and thoroughly smudge the bed. You can also sprinkle salt on the mattress and allow it to remain there for 24 hours before removal. Salt is an excellent purifier and can absorb large amounts of old or stagnant energy. Never eat salt that has been used for Space Clearing purposes.

If you're recently divorced but are still sleeping on the same bed you shared with your spouse, it's wise to get a new mattress. Replacing your mattress is also recommended after a serious illness, a death, or any other traumatic event. Your mattress can retain the energy of your emotions, which can affect you on a subconscious level while you're sleeping.

Bells

Bells are excellent tools to use for Space Clearing. They have the ability to dispel accumulated, stagnant energy by producing a sound that permeates the molecules of a space. The resonating tone of a bell increases the flow of energy and restores vibrational balance. Long after you can no longer physically hear the sound of a bell, its subtle vibrations continue to pervade a space in an almost mystical manner.

Throughout history, bells have often been associated with mysticism. In some cultures, they were made of seven metals, each of which was thought to carry the energy of a different planet—an idea originally postulated by Aristotle. When a bell of seven metals was rung, it was believed that it generated universal forces capable of aligning the cosmos. In many traditions, the ringing of bells was thought to drive away harmful sprits and negative energy.

Types of Bells

Tibetan Bells: Currently, one of the best (and easiest to obtain) bells to use for Space Clearing is the Tibetan bell, called a *ghanta*. Originating in Tibet, these highly symbolic bells are now created in India and Nepal by Tibetan refugees. Every part of a Tibetan bell is symbolic. The bell is always accompanied by a small metal object called a *dorje*. The *dorje* represents the male principle, power, salvation, and the vitality of lightning. The bell itself represents the feminine principle, wisdom, and the great void. Together, the *ghanta* and the *dorje* are thought to restore balance in an environment, because they activate the two opposing, yet harmonious, forces in the universe: *yin* and *yang*. To use these two tools together, you ring the bell while keeping the *dorje* in your pocket, on a Blessing Tray, or in your hand. They create a sacred unity that can harmonize the two primordial creative forces of life.

Frightening faces are sometimes imprinted on the surface of Tibetan bells. Laden with meaning, these images of gods and goddesses are intended to dispel forces of evil and darkness. On top of the bell there is a mandala of eight lotus leaves, symbolizing the voices of the gods. Along the bottom edge of the bell are images of 51 *dorjes*, representing 51 challenges that can be resolved through the ringing of the bell. Tibetan bells can also be played by circling a wooden mallet around the circumference of the bell. Playing the bell in this way creates a powerful vibrating sound that resonates in all directions.

❧ *Balinese Bells:*

Some of the best bells in the world for Space Clearing come from Bali. These illustrious bells not only have a superior tone, but part of their potency also stems from the fact that their creation is synchronized with the phases of the moon, and with prayers and blessings offered at each step of the process. Making a bell can take two months or longer, but on the auspicious day when it's finally complete, a beautiful consecration ceremony calls life into the newborn bell.

❧ *Other Bells:*   Different bells have different energies, based on the metals they are made from and their place of origin. However, any bell can be used for Space Clearing if you feel a sense of connection with it and love its sound. Use your intuition to find the bell that is right for you.

Assessing Energy with a Bell

Bells can be used to assess the energy of a room before you clear it. As you ring a bell in various parts of a room, you may notice places where the bell sounds crisp, and areas where it sounds muffled. A crisp sound usually indicates clear energy; a dull sound usually means that there is some stagnant or negative energy present.

Purification with a Bell

Stand at the entrance to the room. Hold the bell next to your heart, and imagine pure joy and love filling it. Then slowly begin to walk around the circumference of the room. As you walk, ring or strike the bell, and know that your intention is being carried on the vibrations of sound into every corner of the space.

Blessing with a Bell

When the purification stage is complete, the room should seem sparkling and bright. Then, in order to call forth angels, blessings, and spiritual life force into the room, ring the bell three times. Wait until the last ring has completely stilled; then, in the moment of silence that follows, imagine golden light filling the entire space. The room has now been blessed.

Benzoin

This gum resin incense is excellent to use for deep purification of a space and for calling forth spiritual blessings. It is used in some religious ceremonies, such as those of the Greek Orthodox Church, although rarely in Roman Catholic churches. It has a unique ability to attract positive spiritual forces. When burned on a charcoal briquette together with frankincense, each resin heightens the effect of the other and creates a peak sacred energy in a space.

Blessing Altar

The Blessing Altar acts as a spiritual center for your Space Clearing. It is created anew each time you perform a Space Clearing, and is disassembled afterwards. It is the place where you begin your clearing with meditation, and where you end it with a prayer. This altar sets and grounds the energy for everything you do in your ceremony; therefore, it's very important. It should be simple and beautiful.

To set up the Blessing Altar, first lay out a beautiful cloth somewhere near the entrance to your home or in a central location. You can use a small table for this, such as a coffee table. It can also be laid out on a counter top or even on a clean floor or rug. A candle placed in the center of the Altar Cloth consecrates the space. You may also want to create a small arrangement of flowers and incense, or make a mandala-like circle of special stones, shells, or flowers to focus the energy of your Space Clearing. Next, lay out all of the tools you will be using in your clearing on or around the Altar Cloth.

Take time to meditate at the Blessing Altar before you begin your clearing, and once again when you have completed your ceremony. Begin by clearly visualizing your intention for the Space Clearing. Offer prayers for the inhabitants of your home and for yourself. Call in the energy of angels or other totems or spirit helpers that have meaning for you. Still your thoughts, and let the peace and beauty of the Blessing Altar enter into your heart and soul.

At the conclusion of your Space Clearing, it's *absolutely essential* that you take time at the Blessing Altar to ground and integrate the Space Clearing that you've performed. Failure to do so can sometimes lead to problems following the clearing. For example, the people in your home might experience emotional upheaval, or there could be physical problems as a result. Such problems sometimes manifest in the electrical or plumbing systems of the home. Doing a Space Clearing and then failing to integrate the energy when you're done is a bit like stirring up a stagnant pond without allowing it time to settle and become clear again afterwards. Space Clearing can stir up old, dormant energies, so it's important to smooth them over afterwards.

Breath

The use of breath in Space Clearing is one of the oldest, simplest, and most powerful techniques. Ancient shamans controlled their breathing in order to enter altered states of consciousness, where they received guidance for their people. Breath is life, and it has the power to transform and heal. Medicine men and women, devotees, mystics, and visionaries have all used the knowledge of this truth in their practices since the earliest times.

One Space Clearing method using breath is known as the *Breath of God*. It is an excellent way to clear a room. To use this technique, first take a deep breath. Fully expand your lungs, and slowly exhale, through your mouth, into each of the four corners of the room. Use your hands to move your breath in the direction you're clearing. Use one large breath for each direction. Or, you can blow into each of the cardinal four directions—east, south, west, and north—rather than the four corners of the room. Each method is equally effective. Choose the one that feels right for you.

You can also use short, sharp breaths exhaled in the four directions, instead of one long, slow breath. Short breaths are usually better for breaking up heavy, stagnant energy, while long breaths are preferred for smoothing and uplifting energy.

A B C D E F G H I J K L M N O P Q R S T U V W X Y Z

C

Camphor

Camphor is excellent for freeing up very stagnant or stuck energy. Although its very powerful smell may be too strong for some, camphor is particularly useful in situations where milder agents won't do the trick. Older homes that have accumulated a great deal of negative energy over many years or through tragic circumstances can be effectively cleared with camphor. Natural camphor is highly superior to synthetic camphor, which is more readily available than the natural kind. Camphor is a crystalline resin that can be burned on a charcoal briquette or in combination with other incense resins, or it can be burned on its own in a fireproof dish.

Candles

Candles have been universal metaphors for life and energy for centuries. The candle's flame serves as a powerful focus for intention and meditation. It can also help activate your own inner fire and life force. A magical moment occurs when a candle is lit. As the match ignites the wick, focus your intention and know that it will fill the space you're clearing with light, warmth, and fresh energy.

Place a candle in the center of your Blessing Altar to ground the energy of your clearing. Keeping a candle burning in a room as you cleanse it will also deepen the purification that you're doing there. The light of the candle will also sustain and energize you. Although any kind of candle can be used, beeswax candles carry a softer, smoother, and more radiant energy than petroleum-based candles. Also, you might want to consider using a candle that contains essential oil. Candles with pine, rosemary, lemon, lime, tea tree, or eucalyptus oil are all very purifying.

Always take appropriate precautions to avoid any fires when you're using candles. Make sure that they're in a secure place with no flammable items nearby, and out of the way of children and pets. Never leave a burning candle unattended unless it's in a flameproof container and in a completely secure place. Never assume that such precautions will be adequate in a home with young children, as nearly all kids are drawn to the beauty and warmth of burning candles.

Casting

Casting is a potent Space Clearing method that's often performed using water or salt. It's especially effective in dwellings that have very heavy or negative energy. To cast with salt, take a bowl with salt that has been left in the sun for several hours. Gather some of this salt in your hand and cast it throughout each room of the home with the intent of casting out the dark and bringing in the light. This method must be done in a precise way, so that with every toss of the salt you're also *clearly focused on your intent* of banishing negativity.

Casting can also be done by taking a bowl of holy water and using your fingertips, a sprig of an herb, such as rosemary, or a small sprig of pine or cedar needles. Dip your fingers or the sprig into the water, and cast the water in all directions in each room. (Although flowers can be used to sprinkle water for blessings, do not use flowers for water casting.) After you have cast energy in this way, a room will sparkle with energy and light.

Cedar

Cedar needles are a gift to any Space Clearer. They can be used when fresh to cast holy water, and they can be used when dried to burn and create cedar smoke, which is very purifying. Native Americans of the southern woodlands used cedar exclusively to purify their homes and bodies of negative energy. They believed that it had a cleansing power that surpassed anything else.

Chakras

The human body houses seven energy centers called *chakras*, which are situated along a line running from the base of the spine to the crown of the head. When these energy centers are balanced, an individual feels stabilized and well. At the conclusion of any Space Clearing ceremony, it's important to cleanse and bless the individuals who live in the home as well. One way to do this is to place stones or gemstones, such as quartz crystals, on the *chakras* of the body while a person is lying in a supine position. Doing so creates a protective web of energy around the individual as you Space Clear them. It also deepens the effects of the Space Clearing.

To perform this kind of healing ceremony, first have the individual lie down. Place stones on the body in the following way: Place one stone on top of the pubic bone. Place the second stone on the center of the abdomen. Place the third stone on the solar plexus. The fourth stone is placed in the center of the chest. Place the fifth stone on the throat, and the sixth on the center of the forehead. The seventh and final stone is placed on the floor or bed, just above the top of the head. Once you've carefully positioned all of these seven stones on the *chakras*, then take other stones and place them around the body. Next, you will gently take the tool that you used for Space Clearing the home, such as a drum, bell, or sage smoke, and wave that tool up and down the person's body until they feel lighter and clearer. This is a wonderful way to end any Space Clearing.

Chanting

Chanting combines the power of your voice with sacred words. In ancient times, sages and mystics understood the great power of words. They believed that chants could have a magical effect on an environment. Chants were created to combine the powerful meaning of a word with a particular vibration of a sound. When you chant a traditional mantra, such as the word *aum* or *om*, it overrides the normal chatter of your brain. It allows you to become much more focused in your work and creates a mystical resonance that can dramatically and positively influence an environment.

You can recreate this tradition by repetitively chanting words that have a special meaning for you. For example, you could chant the word *home* over and over again in your Space Clearing, with the intention that each of the occupants of your household will feel at home with themselves wherever they are.

Charcoal

A charcoal briquette can be used to burn resins such as frankincense and myrrh, aromatic woods such as sandalwood, or herbs such as juniper or sage. These substances are all excellent for Space Clearing and smudging a room. There is something very magical about the practice of smudging, and the smoke produced immediately fills a space with a special sense of the sacred, the ancient, and the profound.

To call upon the alchemy of fire and air, first light a small charcoal tablet or briquette with a candle or lighter. Then place it in a deep bowl filled halfway with sand, salt, or earth. This protective layer is very important because it insulates the bowl from the heat of the charcoal. You will want to use small metal tongs to hold the charcoal briquette when you light it, because it will be become extremely hot very quickly. The charcoal sometimes emits sparks as well, so be sure to light it in a safe place away from anything that could catch fire from a stray spark.

Once the charcoal tablet is burning in the fireproof bowl, you can place herbs or resinous incense on it with the tongs or with metal chopsticks. Usually this creates a volume of smoke. Carefully carry the bowl into each room so that the smoke fills every corner of the home. As you work, hold the thought that the smoke is purifying and blessing everything that it touches. Be aware of where smoke detectors are located in the home, and direct your smudging away from them to prevent unwanted distractions.

When you're burning resins, you can gently fan them with a feather or fan. However, if you are using loose herbs, such as sage leaves, it's often best to simply let them burn rather than fanning them. This is because the movement of the feather can cause smoldering leaves to fly out of the bowl, thus creating a potential fire hazard. So be careful. Once you've completed your Space Clearing, lift the charcoal briquette out of the bowl with your metal tongs, and extinguish it in a container of water.

Chi

Within every space, there is a subtle energy field that flows like water. In the Orient, this energy flow is called *chi,* which is the life force in all things. In both Feng Shui and Space Clearing, the goal is to create a healthy, strong, and relaxed flow of *chi* throughout the home. It should not be too fast or stagnant, but rather a vital stream of energy gently flowing without disruption. Space Clearing clears out stagnant pools of energy so that *chi* can once again flow freely, full of healing life force.

If *chi* in a home is not balanced, it is either too *yin* (slow) or too *yang* (fast). For example, after a sickness or death of a loved one, the energy of a home often becomes sluggish and heavy, or *yin* in nature. To dispel the listless energy and restore balance in the area, Space Clearing techniques should be *yang* in nature—that is, vibrant and quick moving. Drums and gongs are excellent tools to use in such a case. On the other hand, if the energy of a space feels agitated, perhaps as a result of an argument, the use of *yin* techniques and tools, such as a softly chanted mantra or a crystal singing bowl, can smooth and soothe the energy to create a sense of tranquility and calm.

Chimes

Hand-held chimes create a very clear and focused sound that is excellent for Space Clearing. Strike the chimes sharply to create vibrations that can pierce even the dullest pools of energy. After you strike a chime, move it as though you were using a paintbrush, with long, broad strokes to diffuse the sound throughout an area. The energy flows created by chimes are celestial and sublime.

Clapping

Your hands are a simple set of Space Clearing tools that you will never be without. If you're stuck someplace that needs clearing and you have none of your usual equipment, use your hands. Clap them together, making brisk and sharp claps. Circle the room facing the wall, clapping as you go. Pay particular attention to the corners, where stagnant energy often accumulates. When you find a place where your clapping sounds muffled, continue to clap until you get a crisp, clear sound. When this happens, you will know that the energy is clear.

Click Sticks

Used by many native cultures, such as the Aborigines in Australia and by some African tribes, click sticks are an easy, highly effective tool you can use for clearing a room. Take two sticks and strike them together in a rhythmic way. Let the energy of the room flow through you to find the best pace and rhythm. Move around the room, striking the sticks high and low and paying attention to any place where the sound seems dull. When you've completed your circle, you should notice a distinct difference in the energy of the room.

It's fairly easy to make your own click sticks (also sometimes called "clap sticks") from wooden dowels or two sticks you find in nature. They can be left plain, painted, or carved with symbols that are sacred to you. The most important thing is the sound created by the sticks. It should be sharp and crisp.

Clutter

Clutter can block the flow of life-force energy in a home. It can represent a fear of the future, or an inability to let go of the past and live in the present. Uncompleted projects that accumulate in the basement or garage can burden us with guilt and keep us from doing things we would enjoy so much more. Either complete them or get rid of them. Clutter in your home can symbolically represent blockages in your life. The good news is that when you get rid of the clutter, often you will find that the obstacles it represents seem to just melt away, too!

Before doing any Space Clearing, it's best to do a thorough housecleaning, followed by a de-clutter session. A simple rule of thumb is: *If you don't love it or use it, get rid of it!* You'll be amazed by how much freer you'll feel. When your home is free of clutter, the magic and power of Space Clearing is increased exponentially.

Consecrating Your Tools

The tools you use in your clearing will be much more powerful if you consecrate them before you begin. One of the ways to do this is to hold them in a plume of smoke. As the smoke envelops the instrument you will use, know that you're symbolically cleansing and purifying it, dedicating it to the work that you're going to do. Or, you can place your tools in the sunshine for a few hours to be purified and consecrated by the golden rays of the sun.

Corners

"Evil dwells in the corners," is an expression used in native cultures throughout the world. Although evil doesn't necessarily lurk in the corners of our homes, it is certainly the place where stagnant energy accumulates. Energy flows like water throughout our residences. One way to better grasp this idea is to imagine a stream of water flowing through your home. Debris carried by the water would tend to accumulate in the nooks, crannies, and corners of a room. The free flow of psychic energy also tends to get stuck in these areas, so it's important to pay special attention to the corners in your Space Clearing.

Dance

Sacred dance is an ancient and very beautiful method for transforming the energy of an environment. It's not necessary to be a professional dancer (or even a very accomplished one) to use dance to clear a room. Simply put on some music that touches your heart—music that feels like it opens you up and activates your energy field. To effectively clear a space, hold the intention for your Space Clearing in your soul as you listen to the music. Then slowly allow your intent to move through you as you begin to "dance the room." Let the music direct all of you—body, legs, head, arms, and hands—in this way you will begin to clear the energy of the space. Let yourself merge with the music as you dispel the stagnant energy and invite in new and beneficial *chi*. As you dance, visualize beautiful, fresh, crystal clear energy swirling in eddies throughout the room, following the graceful power of your dancing movements.

Doors

Doors can symbolize portals into other realities, and thus have been recognized as universal metaphors for transformation throughout the ages. In Space Clearing, we pay particular attention to the doors of a home. The front door into a home sets the energy for the home; therefore, it's very important in Space Clearing. The front door also represents the transition point between the inner and outer realms in life. In traditional Feng Shui and Space Clearing, doors are considered to be the mouth of the home and the place where *chi* first enters. As a result, a door is the best place to begin your Space Clearing ceremony. It's also the place where you will return to complete your ceremony to enclose and seal the positive energy that you've generated.

The inner doors into each room are also important because they set the energy for each individual room. Ideally, all the doors in your home should be able to open freely and not be blocked by clutter or debris. They shouldn't squeak or be difficult to open.

Dowsing

Dowsing is a very effective diagnostic tool you can use in your Space Clearing. A dowsing rod or pendulum can be used as a highly sensitive tool to discover stagnant energy in a room. Dowsing can help you determine which areas of a home or office are in particular need of clearing.

If you're using the pendulum method of dowsing, you can ask *yes* or *no* questions about the home, and then watch the movements of the pendulum to discover the answers to your questions. To use this technique, hold a small pendulum so that it can swing freely from your hand. Then ask a question to which you already know the answer—for example, "Am I a woman?" Note whether the pendulum moves on a horizontal or vertical axis in response to your question. This will let you know which way the pendulum moves to indicate a positive or negative response to subsequent questions. You can then proceed to ask the pendulum questions about the space you will be clearing.

You can also use your pendulum to clear energy. Focus your thoughts on the intention that every swirl of the pendulum will contribute to the energy of the room becoming clearer and clearer. As the pendulum swirls in fast concentric circles, the energy in that part of the room will become brighter and lighter.

Dragon's Blood

Dragon's blood is a resinous gum incense that comes from a plant found in Southeast Asia. For thousands of years, people in India have used this remarkable substance in their rituals to dispel and neutralize negative energy. It is believed that dragon's blood not only disperses negativity, but also provides a mantle of protective energy. It is a very potent resin that creates a thick black smoke, so it is best added in small qualities to another resin, such as frankincense.

Dragon's blood is often obtained in a powdered form, but it can also come in chunks, from which you can chip off small pieces of the resin. It's a very potent incense to use for removing malignant influences in a home. When placed on a burning charcoal briquette, dragon's blood will bubble a deep red color reminiscent of its name. It's a good idea to open the windows and doors while you're using this resin. Hold the intention that everything that is not needed or beneficial in the home will move out through the windows, following the plumes of smoke, where they will be released into the cleansing breath of the wind.

Drum

The drum is one of the most ancient and powerful of all Space Clearing tools. Drumming connects us to the basic rhythm of life. It activates the primordial pulse of life that we first knew in the womb. The beating of the drum can align a living space to the universal cadence within all things. Cave drawings by early humans indicate that the drum has been a favorite tool of shamans throughout the ages.

When you play a drum for Space Clearing, let the energy of the drum move through you to help you find the rhythm that is right for your ceremony. Begin by holding your drum close to your heart, and visualize love flowing from your heart into the drum. Clearly imagine the desire for your clearing. Rub your hand in a circle around the surface of the drum to warm and greet it, and then slowly begin to beat it. Listen carefully to the sound of the drum as you move throughout the room. Notice any differences in the quality of the sounds produced.

If there are places where the drum sounds dull, pay attention to those areas. Where the beat of the drum sounds thudlike, there is a pool of stagnant energy. Continue to drum in that area until the sound becomes bright and clear. This is an indication that the energy is stronger and is cleared there. Let your drum tell you what to do! When you connect with the spirit of the drum, it can communicate the best cadence to use, the appropriate strength of the beat, and even where to strike its surface. The power of the drum will surge through your being as you open to its consciousness. The rhythm will often vary spontaneously as you move from one area of a room to another. This happens because the drum is intuitively responding to what is needed by the room.

You can also use a drum to magnify a chant. Hold the drum close to your mouth without actually touching it, and chant or tone into it. The sound will broadcast powerfully throughout the room. An excellent drum to use for this technique is the Irish *bodhran* drum, because the thin skin of this drum results in a more powerful vibration. However, other kinds of drums can also be used.

The tension of the head of a drum will fluctuate in response to the humidity and temperature of the surrounding air. If you live in a damp climate and your drum sounds a bit flat, this is natural. You may need to gently warm your drum in front of a fire or over a lamp, taking care not to burn the skin. If your drum sounds like a tin can, it may be too dry. In this case, you can gently mist it with water until the tone you desire is obtained. A drum (and all Space Clearing tools) should be kept in a place of honor, either hung securely on a wall, or stored in a beautiful bag or case.

E

Electromagnetic Fields (EMFs)

Although not a traditional aspect of Space Clearing, electromagnetic fields (EMFs) *do* affect the energy of a home or business. Thus, it is worthwhile to discover where the strongest EMFs are located. Use a Gauss meter to identify where these fields are, and then make sure you're not sleeping or sitting for long periods of time in close proximity to them. Substantial research suggests that spending long periods of time in strong electro-magnetic fields can have a detrimental effect on one's health, so it's absolutely essential to identify the EMFs in your home, and then to position your bed and other furniture so that you're spending as little time as possible close to these potential sources of harm. *Space Clearing will not neutralize the effects of EMFs!*

Energy (Sensing Energy)

Sensing energy is the most basic and essential skill necessary for all phases of Space Clearing. There are a number of excellent ways to sense the energy of a room. One way is to simply walk around an area and notice how it feels. Feelings are often a reliable indication of the energy in a space, because our emotions will be influenced by the energy that we encounter there. You might find that one place makes you feel down and depressed, another area makes you feel dizzy, and yet another causes you to feel agitated.

A more structured variation on this method is to walk around the room in a clockwise direction with your left hand extended toward the wall. Notice any place where your hand seems to feel heavy or tingly or cold. These sensations often occur in response to stagnant energy pools.

You can also use an instrument, such as a drum or bell. Play it in various places in a room, and notice how the sound varies from one spot to another. If the drum sounds thudlike in one area, or the bell sounds dull, you can be sure that this is an indication of stagnant energy or psychic sludge. Similarly, you can sense positive energy in areas where the tone sounds particularly clear or resonant, or where you suddenly feel uplifted, energized, or happy. In an area of clear, fresh energy, you will be able to breathe easier, you will feel more expansive, and sometimes the room will seem brighter. Sensing energy in a room will give you a good indication of where you need to focus your Space Clearing efforts. You should be able to feel a difference before and after you clear an area.

Entrance

The threshold into a home is very important. It sets the energy for the whole residence because it is the first impression that you receive when you enter the dwelling. Therefore, it is very important to pay attention to the objects that are placed here. The entrance has been called the "mouth of the home" because it is the place where energy first comes in. Thus, the threshold forms an energy template that influences everything throughout the home.

The entrance is an excellent place to place positive metaphors. An inspirational picture hung in this location will lift your spirits each time you enter your home. A special statue, such as one of St. Francis or Kwan Yin, the goddess of compassion, would create a template of loving energy. A healthy plant near the front door is also conducive to creating positive energy.

Because the front entrance is so important to the overall energy of the home, it's an ideal location to set up the Blessing Altar for your Space Clearing ceremony. This is the place where you will begin and end your clearing. The front entrance is also one of the best areas in the home to establish a permanent home altar.

Essential Oils

Aromatherapy essential oils are excellent allies to use in your Space Clearing. Each oil brings its own special energy into a space, and there are many books that contain a wealth of information about each of them.

Here are some tips to help you get started: Lemon, lime, rosemary, clary sage, eucalyptus, pine, juniper, and fir are all excellent for cleansing energy. Lavender and bergamot are beneficial for invoking a sense of peace and relaxation. Orange and tangerine ignite a sense of joy, and rose stimulates the healing power of love.

You may want to create a special formula of your own for use in your Space Clearing ceremonies. You can use this mixture either with an oil burner, or combine it with spring water in a spray bottle for misting the air in your home during the clearing. The scent of essential oils can activate the life force of flowers and herbs in your home, bringing the vital qualities associated with them into the energy fields there.

The Magic

of

flowers

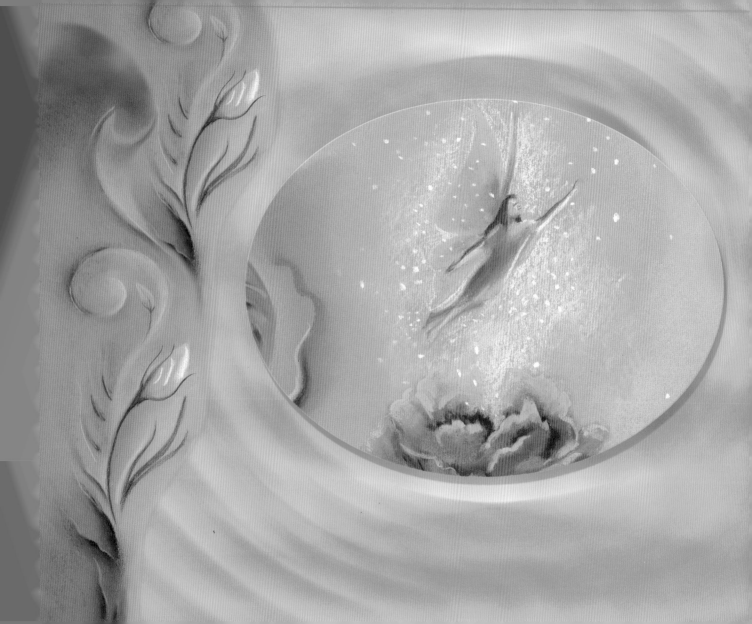

𝓕

Fans

Feather fans, bamboo fans, and paper or fabric fans can all be used with excellent results during a Space Clearing. In ancient times, women sometimes used a quick flick of a fan to avert evil. Similarly, you can use rapid flicks of a fan to transform the energy in your home. Simply moving the fan swiftly over an area with stagnant energy, and then ending with slow, sweeping movements, can facilitate a change for the better. You can also use a folded fan to rap on an object that's out of harmony with its surroundings. Doing so will bring it back into balance.

For example, a few taps with a bamboo fan on a woven basket that somehow just doesn't feel right can often restore its sense of harmony. This method evokes the law of similars. In other words, the energy vibration of the bamboo in the fan is similar to the energy of the woven reed basket, so it responds to the tapping of the fan more readily than it would to the ringing of a bell. Also, to increase the spiritual potency of your fan, you may want to decorate it with beautiful calligraphy or other special symbols that are meaningful to you.

Feathers

Feathers are very sensitive tools to use for both sensing and clearing energy. They've been a favored tool of shamans since the beginning of human history. Because the quill of the feather is an open tube, many cultures have believed that it serves as a channel for prayers and energy. Feathers can also bring the airy energy of the skies, and the freedom of wind and flight into a home.

Because of their delicate attunement to the finer aspects of energy, feathers are useful for all phases of the clearing, from the initial assessment of energy, to the latter stages of clearing and balancing energy. They can be used by themselves to clear a space or in conjunction with smoke. Either way, they lend an energy to your work that is both powerful and gentle. A single feather or a feather fan firmly held in the hand can be flicked in quick, short strokes to break up stagnant energy; while long, graceful movements can smooth out and calm erratic energ;. Always be sure to cleanse your feathers after using them for Space Clearing. This can be done by passing them through sage, cedar, or juniper smoke after you've completed your ceremony.

Clearing a Room with Feathers

To clear a room using a feather, first take some time to connect with the energy of the feather. Hold it next to your heart, and imagine yourself merging with it and connecting to the spirit of the bird from which it came. Then begin with short, flicking movements as you circle the room. Wherever you sense a pooling of stagnant energy, chop into it with the feather to break it up and get it moving. Then make longer, slower, more fluid motions with the feather to create a healthy, balanced, and calm flow of energy throughout the room.

Clearing a Person's Aura with a Feather

After you've completed a Space Clearing, you can use your feather to clear your own energy or that of other household members. The person you're working with can stand, sit, or lie down for this clearing. Begin with short flicking movements, working from head to toe over the entire body. If you come to a place that seems to feel "sticky" or somehow "heavy," this can indicate that the energy is stuck or stagnant there. Concentrate your efforts with the feather in this area, making short, quick movements to break up the energy before you move on. Once you feel the energy beginning to change, switch to long, smooth strokes of the feather to even out the energy. You can also use the feather in a similar way over your own body.

Using Feathers with Smoke

A highly effective way to clear a room is to combine the movements of the feather with the use of smoke. These two elements together create an alchemy of air and fire that's one of the most powerful ways to balance the energy of any room. The natural channeling powers of the feather, combined with the purifying and spiritual properties of the burning incense or herbs, can create a sense of deeply sacred space anywhere.

To activate this alchemy of fire and air, hold a bowl containing sand and the smoking herbs/incense/sage bundle in your nondominant hand. An abalone shell can also be used, but a deep bowl is a practical alternative that can be a little easier to manage. Make sure that the bowl or shell is deep enough to prevent any sparks or burning leaves from flying out of it into the room. You will also want to be sure that the bowl contains enough sand, salt, or earth to insulate it from the heat of the burning herbs so that it doesn't burn your hand. Use the feather in your dominant hand to move the smoke over the body of a person you're clearing, or throughout a room. Use small, flicking motions followed by long, sweeping ones.

Kinds of Feathers

A common type of feather used for Space Clearing is the turkey feather. These feathers are readily available at craft stores and fishing-supply stores in the fly-tying section. Native Americans call the turkey the "giveaway" bird, because it's believed that the turkey embodies the spirit of being of service to others. You can use other feathers for Space Clearing, but please note that governments often have very specific legal restrictions regulating the possession of bird feathers. These laws are intended to protect species that might otherwise go extinct. Out of respect for these animals and our environment, it's essential that you first find out what regulations relate to possession and use of feathers in your area.

The following is a list of some feathers and their attributes. It's not intended to be complete, but only as an aid to help you get started. When trying to decide if a particular feather is right for you, tune in to its energy. Let your intuition tell you which is the best one for you.

❧ *Turkey:* — An outstanding feather for Space Clearing, the turkey feather enhances the power of your work because its spirit is aligned with higher purpose and with helping others.

❧ *Raven:* — Connected to the inner life and secret realms, the feathers of the raven symbolize a deep and powerful energy.

❧ *Eagle and Hawk:* — These feathers call forth the energy of the sun. Their use in Space Clearing brings a soaring and powerful energy to your ceremony.

❧ *Owl:* — Owl feathers are associated with feminine mysteries, the energy of the moon, and ancient wisdom.

❧ *Goose:* — Geese live in highly socialized flocks and mate for life. Their feathers represent loyalty and family ties.

Caring for Feathers

Treating your feathers with the respect they deserve enhances their effectiveness. You will want to keep them in a special place and "feed" them by occasionally sprinkling them with a bit of cornmeal and then shaking it off. Doing so symbolically feeds the spirit of the bird and replenishes the feathers' energy.

Many birds have insect parasites that may be present in feathers. If left untreated, these mites will eventually eat your feathers away and destroy their beauty and usefulness. Storing your feathers in cedar, sage, borax, or tobacco can help prevent this type of degradation.

Forms of Feathers to Use in Space Clearing

Feathers used for Space Clearing come in three traditional forms: single feathers, feather fans, and wings. You can use a single, unadorned feather, or you can decorate it by wrapping the exposed end of the quill with leather or cloth. This, in turn, can be decorated with strips of leather and beads.

Another option is to use a feather fan, which is usually made from several feathers gathered together and secured with a piece of leather or a wooden base. Wings and feather fans have a wider surface for moving energy throughout a room, but are a little less easy to control than a single feather.

Feng Shui

Space Clearing is an important aspect of Feng Shui, because it heightens the effectiveness of Feng Shui. Space Clearing an environment makes all of the Feng Shui cures that have been implemented even more effective. A home can have perfect Feng Shui and excellent furniture placement, but if the energy in the house is stagnant and is filled with residual psychic sludge, it won't feel right. It's only when the space has been purified and blessed that it really begins to shine. Space Clearing has the remarkable ability to take all of the benefits of Feng Shui up to the next level!

Figure-Eight

A sideways figure-eight is the sign of infinity or the sign of the *mobius*. This sign is made in the air with your hand or with a Space Clearing tool to seal the energy that you've created through your ceremony. You make this sign as you finish clearing each room, and also at the very end of your clearing. As you make your final figure-eight, say a blessing. The sign of infinity preserves the blessing and all of the work you've done in the home long after you've finished your clearing there. It also symbolizes that the wonderful energy that has been generated in the room will continue into infinity.

Flower Essences

Flower essences are excellent to use for Space Clearing because they imbue the spiritual properties of the flowers into your home. Each flower essence contains the pure spiritual essence of each individual flower. This is a type of vibrational alchemy that can bring a wonderful, smooth, balanced energy into your home.

Although you can create your own flower essences, usually the highest quality, vibrational flower essences are those that have been created by people who have dedicated their life to this work. Bach Flower Essences, California Flower Essences, Australian Bush Essences, Perelandra Essences, and Alaskan Flower Essences are all reputable companies. The Alaskan Flower and Environmental Essences are particularly beneficial because the Alaskan air is so clean and the land is so unpolluted.

To create a flower essence, the flower is picked at its peak in the early morning hours. There is an attunement with the flower to "ask permission" before it is picked. The flower is then floated in pure spring water while the sun shines down on it. This is done in a meditative state to invite the energy of the flower into the water. Thus, the water becomes infused with the radiant energy of the flower.

When you add a few drops of flower essence to your holy water, it absorbs the qualities of the flower. This kind of water can create a delicate web of energy, which is very healing, and conducive to inviting joy and love into your home. You can sprinkle this water throughout your home, or you can place it in an atomizer to mist from room to room. Which flower essences you use will depend on the kind of energy you want to create. What follows is a partial list of some essences and their qualities to help get you started:

To Call Peace and Serenity into a Home

Chamomile:	calming, soothing, relaxing
Centaury:	stillness, quietness, serenity, wisdom
Cherry Plum:	relaxing, calming, quiet energy
Lavender:	soothing, relieves tension and stress
Mimulus:	minimizes fear and dread
Water Violet:	tranquility, gentle poise, grace

To Awaken Clarity and Mental Focus in a Home

Blackberry:	direct action, decisiveness
Cerato:	ignites confidence, assists with decision making
Clematis:	releases lethargy and initiates focus
Peppermint:	stimulating, increases alertness
Rosemary:	activating, releases mental fog
Shasta Daisy:	synthesis of ideas

To Cleanse Negative Patterns
Out of a Home   (e.g., after a divorce or trauma)

Cayenne: powerful release of the old, catalyst for change

Fireweed: best essence for dispelling old patterns and activating new energy

Gorse: overcoming difficulties

Rescue Remedy: balances energy after trauma, argument, or illness

Sagebrush: cleanses old habits that are no longer appropriate

To Establish a Protective
Shield Around a Home

Garlic: psychic protection for the home

Pennyroyal: dispels negative influences

Yarrow: excellent for shielding outside influences

To Ignite Energy and Vitality

Indian Paintbrush: creativity and life force

Peppermint: stimulating, alert and vital energy

Morning Glory: awakening vigor

Wild Rose: vitality, lively interest in all things

To Summon Spiritual Awakening

Angel's Trumpet: soothing and peaceful; spiritual initiation

Angelica: assists guidance from the Divine realm

Black-Eyed Susan: summons spiritual consciousness

Iris: spiritual integration

Lotus: reopening spiritual consciousness that
has been restricted

Flowers

Flowers can be a magical addition to any Space Clearing, for their delicate smell and colorful petals call positive spiritual energy into a home.

There are four ways that flowers can be used for Space Clearing. First, they can be placed in a beautiful bouquet on the Blessing Altar to sanctify the energy created there. Second, they can be used to create flower offerings to be left in the various rooms of your home during the Space Clearing. Third, the petals of flowers can be used to sprinkle holy water throughout a space. And a fourth way to use flowers during Space Clearing is to adorn yourself or your bells and other tools with them.

Flowers are used in Space Clearing because they are thought to invoke the celestial energy of angels and devas. Each flower has its own special qualities that can be used in your clearing work. The following is a partial list of some common flowers that are excellent for Space Clearing:

❧ *Apple Blossom:*   Associated with new growth, healing, and purification. This flower invokes a sense of renewed hope and faith.

❧ *Chrysanthemum:*   Brings calm and rational energy into the home. Promotes introspection. Good for meditation, and associated with longevity.

❧ *Daffodil:*   Full of joy and acceptance. Radiates light-heartedness, hope, and trust.

Daisy: Exudes feelings of childlike innocence and healing. An open and warm-hearted energy that is full of joy.

Echinacea: Excellent for all healing work. A gentle and incredibly strong feminine energy.

Iris: Full of a delicate sensuality and gentle beauty. Very quiet, dignified energy. Simple and elegant.

Lavender: Brings a calm and relaxing energy to any space.

Lily: Invokes purity and the ideal of perfection. Creates a calm and spiritual feeling in the home.

Lily of the Valley: Invokes a gentle sense of innocence and hope. Aligned with springtime and new life.

Marigold: Full of joyful, strong, and healing energy. Associated with longevity and protection.

Rose: Opens the heart to healing and love. Strengthens life-force energy.

Sunflower: Vibrant, exuberant energy, aligned with the power of the sun, from which it takes its name and spirit.

Tulip: Associated with sensual love. Invokes vitality, hope, and optimism.

Violets: Call forth a very yin, delicate energy. They are full of tenderness and promote trust.

Flower Offerings

Leaving flower offerings in each room of a home seals the energy of a clearing in a beautiful and gentle way. The living presence of the flowers continues to exude love and healing long after your ceremony has ended. Flower offerings are a simple and eloquent expression of Spirit. They can be made easily by taking a small votive candle and placing it in the center of a heatproof dish or saucer. The kinds of candles that come in a small metal holder are best.

Place a small amount of water in the dish, and arrange the flowers around the candle. Sticks of incense can also be included in a flower offering by securing them in the wax of the candle.

Leave your flower offerings in a safe place where children or pets will not disturb them. They should be left in place for at least 24 hours following the clearing, but they need not be removed for as long as the flowers remain fresh and lovely.

Choose flowers, colors, and scents for your arrangement that reflect the energy of your ceremony. For example, if your intention is to create a feeling of peace and relaxation in your home, you might want to create a simple flower offering using blue and white flowers, a white candle, and sprigs of fragrant lavender. Creating flower offerings is fun and highly effective. Use your imagination to create arrangements that are both lovely and meaningful.

Sprinkling Holy Water with Flowers

A very traditional way to use flowers for Space Clearing is to grasp the flower head in the tips of your fingers and dip the flower into holy water, which you can lightly sprinkle throughout your home. This combines the subtle energy of the flower with the sublime energy of the holy water, thus bringing forth a wonderful blessing. You can also Space Clear the energy of other individuals in this manner by lightly sprinkling them with flowers laden with holy water. Marigolds and carnations are excellent to use for this purpose, because they hold the water in their folds.

Adorning Yourself with Flowers

If you're doing a very special Space Clearing ceremony, you might wish to adorn yourself with flowers to honor the sacredness of the occasion. Wearing a wreath of flowers in your hair or wearing a beautiful lei is a traditional way of aligning yourself with the powerful, gentle energies of the flower kingdom. The flowers create a delicate web of light and energy that will surround you as you work, lending all your thoughts and actions a special grace and beauty.

Decorating Your Bells with Flowers

In many traditions, the bells used for Space Clearing are honored by adorning them with flowers. Many bells have openings in their tops or handles through which you can gently lace the stems of flowers. When you decorate your bell in this way, the energy of its sound is enhanced by the presence of the flowers. Other tools used in your clearing can also be adorned with flowers to bring grace and beauty to the work that you do.

Four Directions

Space Clearing is traditionally performed either by orienting your actions in relation to the door of each room and the four corners within, or in relation to the four cardinal directions. In Native American tradition, the Four Directions are of paramount importance. These directions are points on the Medicine Wheel, the great symbolic wheel that encompasses all of life. Each direction is associated with one of the four seasons and with the different phases of human life.

East is the direction of new beginnings, springtime, the rising sun, and innocence. South is the direction of summer, warmth, and the rapid growth of childhood. West is the direction associated with autumn and the fruitful time between the teen years and adulthood. North is the direction of winter, going within, and the elders. If you choose to orient your Space Clearing according to the Four Directions, begin each room in the east, the place of new beginnings, and then circle the room from there.

You can call on the spirits of the Four Directions to help you in your clearing work. Take a moment and close your eyes. Still your mind, and imagine your feet touching the earth beneath you. Know that you are a child of Mother Nature, and that all things on Earth are a part of her and a part of you.

Turn to face the east. Ask the spirit of the east to be with you in your Space Clearing. In your mind's eye, watch the rising of the sun as it emerges from the rim of the world each morning. Know that this is the place of new beginnings, hope, innocence, and renewal. Ask the spirit of the east to bring these qualities to your home.

Next, turn to face the south. Ask the spirit of the south to be with you in your ceremony. Feel the warmth of the south as its gentle breezes caress you. Know that this is the direction of summer, growth, and joy. Ask the spirit of the south to fill your clearing with these qualities.

Then turn to the west. Ask the spirit of the west to come into your home. See the warmth of the late afternoon sun as it fills a golden field of ripe wheat with its radiant rays. Know that this is the direction of achievement, fulfillment, and deep satisfaction. Ask the spirit of the west to bring the abundance of the harvest to your home.

Last, turn toward the north. Ask the spirit of the north to be with you as you work. Imagine the magic of small seeds lying dormant in the rich and nurturing bosom of the Earth Mother. Know that this is the direction where dreams are planted, and where body and mind rest in preparation for the exuberant growth of springtime. This is the place of the elders. Ask the spirit of the north to fill your home with wisdom, strength, and deeply grounded energy.

Still your thoughts. Feel your spirit rising up to the heavens, even as your body remains fully grounded in the energy of your Mother, the Earth. Give thanks for all you *have* received and all you *will* receive. Know that the energy of the Four Directions will be with you as you work.

Four Elements

The elements of air, water, fire, and earth were honored by Native American peoples, as well as by other native cultures throughout the world. Also, the ancient people of Greece, Rome, and India—as well as the ancient Celts and Vikings—all honored the four elements. When we honor the four elements, we are honoring four aspects of nature. This is very important in Space Clearing, because not only are you breaking up stagnant energy, you're also invoking the positive energy of nature into your home.

The element of air brings the clarity and freedom of the winds into your home. Water is necessary for all life. When you activate the water principle in your home, you're bringing a primal source of healing, regeneration, and creativity there. The element of fire contains the power of transformation, while the earth element brings grounding and balance.

In your Space Clearing ceremony, it's important to honor each of the sacred elements. You can do so by placing objects on your Blessing Altar that honor the four elements. For example, a feather represents the spirit of air. A candle represents the spirit of fire. A bowl of holy water calls forth the spirit of water, while salt honors the earth element. All of these objects can be used in the clearing, thus inviting the energy of the elements of nature into your home.

Frankincense

Frankincense is a sacred substance that has been used for Space Clearing since earliest human history. It is a resin that is harvested from small trees that grow in the deserts of Arabia. Frankincense is a natural disinfectant and insecticide. It can assist the healing of wounds, improve circulation, and reduce infection. Its rich and aromatic scent combines with this energy of healing to create a uniquely precious substance that has been highly valued by people everywhere since ancient times. Its unique qualities make frankincense an ideal tool for Space Clearing. It can immediately dispel the negativity that remains in a room following an argument. It has been used in sick rooms, churches, and in many other places where people have gathered for thousands of years precisely because of its power and effectiveness.

The scent of natural frankincense varies depending on the kind of tree it was harvested from. There are 25 different varieties of frankincense trees, although most of these are not commercially available. Frankincense is frequently combined with a number of other substances, such as cinnamon, myrrh, benzoin, and dried flowers and herbs to create rich and aromatic incense blends. Its use around the world and throughout the ages has continued uninterrupted into our own time. Its heavenly scent unites humans with the realm of Spirit. Even used alone, frankincense can turn an ordinary room into a haven of mystery, intuitive knowledge, and sacred space.

G

Ghosts

Ghosts are sometimes referred to as earthbound spirits, which is probably a better way of describing them. These are souls who for one reason or another have failed to make their journey all the way to the other side. Perhaps they have issues that they failed to complete during their lives here on Earth, or they may be unable to sever connections with a particular person. Special Space Clearing ceremonies can free these earthbound spirits and enable them to travel onward to a place of infinite light and joy.

The most important thing to remember when working with earthbound spirits is that they are souls who deserve your compassion. Ghosts can't hurt you unless you act on your fear. If you're afraid of them, your emotions can serve to intensify their own fear, which in turn can make you feel even more wary. To break free of this spiral effect, just remember that you are there to assist the ghost. Tell it

Water and Sound

You can also fill a bowl gong partly full of water before you begin to play it as a singing bowl. When you focus your intention for the clearing, the water absorbs this energy and later releases it as you play the gong. The healing properties of the water are magnified out into the room by the vibration of the gong. (This water can also be used for Space Clearing, as it holds the sound energy within its molecular structure.)

Always be sure to thoroughly dry the gong with a soft cloth after using it in this way. Not only is this care necessary for maintaining the beautiful patina surface of the gong, but it also honors and cares for the spirit of the gong.

Grounding

It's absolutely necessary to take time to ground yourself and become centered before undertaking any Space Clearing ceremonies. It isn't possible to overstate the importance of this step. Space Clearing is a very powerful practice that can achieve wonderful results, but the inherent power that is utilized can also result in an imbalance if you go into the process without feeling centered and sure of yourself. Go slowly. Breathe deeply. Take time to meditate and feel at one with the earth before you begin.

To help you ground before any clearing, take a bath to which you add either natural rock salt or Epsom salts. Salt comes from the earth, and it has remarkable grounding powers. Also, taking a salt bath following a clearing will cleanse your aura and release any residual negative energy that you may have accumulated during your clearing work.

As you're working in your home, having a pinch of salt or a grounding stone in your pocket will also help you maintain your sense of focus and calm as you perform the ceremony. Hematite is an excellent stone to use, and so are iron pyrite, black obsidian, and black onyx. These stones have a remarkably balanced energy that facilitates feeling grounded.

It's also very important to ground the home itself once you're done with your Space Clearing. If you fail to do so, then the clearing may result in a great deal of emotional or physical upheaval for the residents of the home. Sealing your house with the sign of infinity helps to ground the clearing. To do so, make a sideways figure-eight sign with your hand in the air when you complete your ceremony. Saying prayers and blessings at the Blessing Altar at the conclusion of your clearing is also an important step to take in order to ground the energy and leave your home in a state of calm grace.

Guardian Spirits

Traditionally, when medicine men and women performed Space Clearing ceremonies, they would call upon guardians from the spirit world. This is something that you can do as well to deepen the effect of your rituals and ceremonies. You might choose to call upon your ancestors, angels, or spirit guides for assistance. Many people have also found it very helpful to call for help from their special totem animals. In some ancient traditions, a Space Clearer would call upon the spirit of the house or the spirit of the surrounding land for guidance. In other cultures, the shaman prays for the Creator or the Spirit of Nature to help with the clearing. Just do whatever feels right to you. No matter what helpers you invoke, you will find that your Space Clearing work is infused with a sacred spirit that empowers you beyond what you could ever accomplish alone. When you're assisted by those in the realm of spirit, miracles occur!

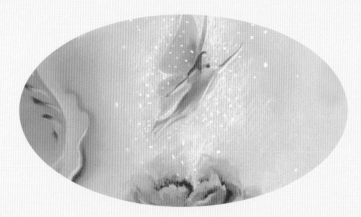

Harmony Balls

Harmony Balls, also called Mayan balls or Druid balls, release a delicate, almost fairylike essence into a room. They are especially beneficial to use after you've already cleared out all of the heavy or negative energy with other Space Clearing tools. For instance, you might begin your ceremony with a gong or large bell, and after you've completely cleared the room with this instrument, you could finish it off with Harmony Balls. Their airy tinkling creates a feeling of shimmering light and leaves a sense of lightness and joy everywhere. Before you begin to use them, hold the Harmony Balls in your hands and imagine that you're filling them with prayers and love and light. Then as you begin to gently shake them around the room, know that these prayers and all of your intentions are being dispersed throughout the room like sparkling beams of light.

Herbs

The use of herbs for Space Clearing goes back to the beginning of time. Every shaman was schooled in the uses of herbs for healing, for spells, and for the clearing of negative energy.

It's important to note that fresh herbs are much more potent than dried ones. For Space Clearing, you can either have a bunch of fresh herbs on your Blessing Altar to bring their vital energy to the altar, or you can use a tightly bound bunch, such as rosemary, to flick throughout your home to dispel stagnant energy. Also, you can take a small sprig of thyme, or whatever plant you decide is right, and then dip its leaves into a small bowl of holy water. Walk around the room you're clearing and gently flick the sprig of herb in the direction of any negative or stagnant energy you encounter. This kind of clearing with fresh herbs creates very healthy energy in a home, and is especially useful for restoring balance and well-being after a period of extended illness or depression.

Dried herbs are often used for burning to create cleansing smoke that can penetrate every part of a room and a home. In the United States, sage is the most commonly used dried herb for Space Clearing, but in other countries, other indigenous dried herbs are used. As a precaution, only burn herbs that have been used traditionally for cleansing, as some emit a toxin when burned. There are many excellent reference books on the different properties of various plants. You can refer to one of these in order to decide which plants will be best for the ceremony that you plan to create. Here is a short list to give you a head start:

A B C D E F G **H** I J K L M N O P Q R S T U V W X Y Z

❧ _Lavender:_	This gentle herb creates a feeling of peace and loveliness wherever it is used. It's especially good for areas that are overly yang.
❧ _Rosemary:_	This is an ancient herb traditionally used in many healing ceremonies and for protection. Rosemary is also very helpful for mental clarity.
❧ _Sage:_	This is the traditional choice for many Native American ceremonies. Sage is associated with purity and spirit. When used for smudging, it is a very powerful cleansing agent in Space Clearing.

Holy Water

Water is considered to be "holy" when it has been specially consecrated for use in ceremonies. It can be sprinkled or misted throughout a home or dwelling. It can also be placed in the center of any room being cleared to absorb and neutralize any stagnant energy released during the clearing.

Holy water is traditionally obtained from a church or shrine, but you can also create your own. The most powerful holy water is created when an individual, who is very focused and loving, instills the water with prayers, care, and love.

To create your own holy water, you must first create a base fluid. This can be done in a number of ways. Water collected from a natural spring carries a special power and is excellent for creating a base. Rainwater is filled with the energy of the heavens, and can also be used as your base. If you're unable to travel to a natural spring or collect rainwater, you can use noncarbonated spring water that has been bottled at the source. Or, ocean water can be used, as it combines the power of water with that of salt. However, you must be careful when using holy water created from seawater; do not use it anywhere where its salt content could damage the materials with which it comes into contact. Here are some other ways to create your holy water base.

Solar water: Place a bowl of water in a sunny location where it can be fully penetrated by the rays of the sun for at least three to five hours. Outdoors is preferable, but a sunny windowsill will do just as well. Solar water is full of the radiant, happy, life-giving energy of the sun. It is yang in nature and excellent for creating a happy, outgoing kind of enegy. It's great to use in a kitchen, living room, and dining room.

Moon water: Lunar water is created by placing a bowl of water outside on a moonlit night. The full moon is the most powerful, but other phases of the moon are good as well. Moon water has a very soft, yin nature, and is good for a bedroom, study, or meditation room for reflection, introspection, and healing.

Star water: This water is created by allowing water to be charged with the energy of the heavens on a clear night. It has a shimmering, magical feel to it that is full of light and joy. It's excellent to use in the bedroom for enhancing dreams and for bringing a feeling of rapture to life.

Rainbow water: This is a magical kind of holy water, especially if you're lucky enough to leave your water outdoors in the presence of a real rainbow! You can also create rainbow water using a prism or crystal to create the spectrum of colors in the bowl of water. Rainbow water creates the energy from which miracles are born. And if you can cap that occurs during a rainbow, this water is a wonderful base.

Flower-infused water: To create a very special and pure kind of holy water, you can add a few drops of flower essence to it. It will then be infused with the special qualities of the flower from which it came. You can also float a flower in a bowl of water left for 20 minutes in the morning sun. Flower water has a childlike innocence. It exudes a very light energy in addition to the individual flower characteristics.

Rainwater: Water collected from the clouds has a gentleness unlike any other water. It is excellent to use for healing and for emotional cleansing.

Crystal water: Place clean quartz crystals into a bowl of water in the sun, or in a sunny window, and know that they're infusing the water with vibrant crystalline energy.

ᔓ *Mineral water:* Place the mineral or minerals that contain the qualities that you would like for your Space Clearing into a clear bowl of water. Leave this undisturbed for at least three hours to infuse the water with the qualities of the minerals. For example, if you want to bring more love into your home, you might place a piece of rose quartz into a bowl of water to elicit the loving qualities associated with rose quartz.

After you've created your holy water base, the next step is to place your hands over it and allow yourself to become a sacred vessel for light, love, and energy. Imagine that radiant light is pouring through you, filling the water with vitality and life force. Add your heartfelt prayers, and your base water now becomes holy water, which you can use in your Space Clearing. After your ceremony, pour any water that is left on the ground, thus freeing its energy so that it can return to its source.

I

Incense

The image of a plume of incense smoke rising upwards is one that conveys an immediate sense of peace and contemplation. Incense has traditionally been used from ancient times to the present, as a medium to carry prayers to heaven. Messages to the unseen travel on the path of the smoke, and blessings and answers are received in return.

Incense comes from all over the world. The range of scents available is as broad and exciting as the many different cultures that they originate from. Choosing which types of incense to use can feel a little confusing sometimes, so a few general prin-ciples can be helpful. First of all, obtain incense made from natural materials. Scents containing artificial chemicals and dyes are not as healthy as natural ones, and they don't have the same spiritual power for shifting energy in a home. Also, whenever you're burning anything in a ceremony, be sure you're taking proper precautions to avoid starting a fire. The following is a short list of some excellent kinds of incense you can use in your clearing:

<dl>

❧ *Cedar:*   Used in ancient Egypt, this wonderfully warm incense has been used all around the world, including the ceremonies of the Native Americans. Its fresh and woody smell creates a quick and intimate connection to the spirit of nature. It is very cleansing.

❧ *Frankincense:*   This ancient and mystical scent has been universally used for Space Clearing since earliest times. A resin harvested from trees grown in Arabian deserts, frankincense is one of the richest and most evocative of all the incenses. It is excellent for purifying any space, and is useful for creating powerful shifts in energy fields.

❧ *Myrrh:*   This incense comes from trees in India that are similar to the frankincense trees of Arabia. Used in India as an Ayurvedic remedy to increase energy, it can increase vitality and energy in a home as well.

❧ *Patchouli:*   This incense has a remarkable and highly sensual smell that lends a sense of earthy passion to any space where it's burned. It's particularly useful for shifting energy in a dwelling that is very cold or lifeless in nature.

</dl>

| *Sage:* | One of the most common plants used for smudging by Native Americans, sage has the ability to clear negative energy very quickly. Its healing properties make it useful in situations where there has been illness, but because the smoke of sage is very strong, not everyone can tolerate its use in enclosed areas. |
| *Sandalwood:* | This wonderful incense comes from India, where it is believed to have great protective properties. It has also been used since ancient times for its healing qualities. Sandalwood is an excellent choice for a wide range of Space Clearing ceremonies. |

Integration

Space Clearing could be called a practice of integration, because what you're really doing when you're clearing a home is creating a state of balance whereby the home, its occupants, and the objects in the home and its surroundings are all properly related to one another. This state of balance is what is meant by integration. When the elements of your home are spiritually integrated, then you won't feel like a stranger in your own space. Your home won't seem like some random dwelling where you've come to reside, but rather, a home for your soul. In such a place, you'll feel supported and loved, and free to let your spirit shine. Your home will radiate love, joy, and spirit, too!

Intention

The best practitioners of Space Clearing have the ability to completely focus and project their intention into a room. They're able to fuse their thoughts and energy field with the energy in an environment and thus shift the way it feels. This is a skill that can be learned. The first step is to become absolutely clear about what it is you're hoping to accomplish. In order to do this, ask yourself what kind of place would really nurture your soul. What are your short- and long-term goals for this area? What are the special needs of each person who will be spending time here? These kinds of questions will help you clearly define exactly what it is you're trying to do.

After you've received your answers, try to find one or two sentences that will sum up your purpose for the clearing. Then close your eyes and imagine that energy is gently rising in your body, up to your heart chakra. As it gains momentum, it surges forth from you and out into the energy field of the room you're clearing. Energy is flowing from you, from your hands, and from the tools you're using to cleanse and purify every area of your environment. Every molecule of space is filled with the power of your intention.

Intuition

Your intuition is your greatest ally in the practice of Space Clearing. In fact, without this gentle force of inner wisdom active within you, Space Clearing is simply not possible. Your intuition is what will help you sense energy and know just what is needed in your home. It is that quiet but insistent voice within you that tells you in which direction beauty and balance lie, where truth is, and what the heart is seeking. Learn to trust this inner voice. It is your friend—not only in clearing homes, but also in every moment of your life.

Invocation

Invocation is the process of calling energy into your home once you've completed clearing the negative energy out of it. It is the finishing touch that completes your clearing, and seals everything you've done beforehand. It sets the energy in such a way that it continues to radiate beneficial effects long after you're done.

When you call energy into your home, be specific. Ask for exactly the kind of energy you hope to establish there. If you're clearing your home in order to create more love there, then call in angels and other loving presences. If you're trying to establish a protective energy that is peaceful and quiet, it might be helpful to call the spirits of totem animal protectors into your home. The energy that you invoke at the end of your clearing will determine how your home will feel, so take some time before you begin to clearly visualize what kind of invocation you'd like to use to end your ceremony.

Prayers are a wonderful part of any invocation. You'll want to both call in energy and helpful spirits into your home, and also thank them for their presence and assistance in the clearing. Open yourself—body, mind, and soul—during the invocation. Let your prayers flow out as you open your heart to receive the blessings that you're calling in to your home.

J

Journal

A journal can be a very powerful adjunct to your Space Clearing practice. It is a safe place to write down your hopes, fears, triumphs, disappointments, and observations about what did or did not work in your ceremonies. A journal can also serve as a window into your subconscious mind. Often dreams, hunches, and seemingly unimportant observations can turn out to be clues to huge discoveries just waiting to be uncovered. A journal is like a portal through which these clues can become apparent to you in your waking, conscious awareness.

Joy

Joy resides at the heart of Space Clearing. It is its essence, its beginning and end. As you clear all negative energy from your home, joy is the feeling that takes its place. And when you return to the Blessing Altar at the conclusion of your ceremony, joy surrounds you like a radiant presence, emanating from each room you've entered.

Juniper

The fragrant needles of the juniper plant have been burned by Native Americans from ancient times to the present. When used for smudging, the evergreen tips of this plant have properties ranging from healing to mental clarification. Juniper is traditionally used in sweat-lodge and peyote ceremonies because of its clearing and cleansing qualities. It has the ability to instantly shift the energy in any environment.

In Nepal, sherpas use the smoke of juniper needles to smudge their ropes and other climbing equipment before making dangerous ascents, because they believe that this protects the equipment from harm.

Karma

The principle of karma is based on balance, and that's what you're trying to create through the practice of Space Clearing. It's important to realize that all negative or stagnant energy comes from somewhere, and when you're clearing it out of your home, it's necessary to replace these elemental forces with light, love, and joy. Restoring the positive energy in your home sets in motion a cycle of karma that begets even more positive energy. The results of your clearing can be like a tiny stone dropped into an enormous pool of energy, with ripples of effect traveling beyond the shores of your wildest imagination.

Keepsake

If you've done a Space Clearing for someone other than yourself, it's a lovely gesture to seal the ceremony with a small gift to the inhabitant(s) of the home or business. A small keepsake can represent their hopes and dreams, or the intention of the clearing. This makes a perfect conclusion to the clearing. You might want to give these individuals a living plant or potted flower, a beautiful stone on which you've inscribed a symbolic word or phrase, or some other memento of this special event that you've created together.

If you're Space Clearing your own home, you and the other members of your household can decide what sort of keepsake would best commemorate the clearing.

Knowledge

The more you learn about energy, focus, tools, and various rituals used around the world, the more powerful your Space Clearing will become. A wise person once said that knowledge is power, and this is certainly true in the practice of Space Clearing. Your path of learning will extend as long as your life, bringing you and the people around you blessings, transformation, and joy!

Land Blessing

Before building a new home, it's valuable to bless the land. Gather family members and friends together, and ceremoniously walk the perimeter of the land. Start at the easternmost point of the land and complete the circle. You might accompany this walk with bells, drums, or prayer wheels. Have each household member hold the intent that good fortune and love will fill the home that will be built on the land. You can also give each person some birdseed to scatter to invite the spirit of nature onto the land. (Traditionally, rice was used, but rice swells in birds' stomachs and can cause health problems for them.) Complete this ceremony with a feast or a shared meal.

Laughter

As the saying goes, *laughter is the best medicine.* This is more than just an old adage. There is profound wisdom embedded in this simple phrase. Heartfelt peals of laughter can clear a room of negative energy faster than almost any other method I know. Research has also shown that laughter is good for your immune system. Similarly, it can fill a space with joy and healthy, revitalized energy. It can instantaneously turn a depressing atmosphere into one where the sun seems to fill every corner—even on a cloudy day.

Law of Similars

If you find that an area of your home is particularly difficult to clear, you can employ the "Law of Similars" to help you. This law operates on the principle that things made of similar materials will have a kind of sympathetic energy between them. For example, if a room has wooden paneling on its walls and a wood floor, then using wooden tools to clear it would result in the most beneficial effects. Wooden click sticks or a drum with a wooden frame would both be good choices for the clearing.

If the energy of your bathroom seems difficult to shift, then use water methods to clear it. If a metal stovepipe leading from a fireplace seems to harbor stagnant energy, then a metal tool such as a bell or chime would be best for clearing the energy there. Or, sage smoke could be used, because the stovepipe is also aligned with smoke, which it normally transports out of the house.

The Law of Similars in Space Clearing can be compared to what happens in human interaction. Often we will listen to a person who has a lot in common with us, when we wouldn't take the same advice from someone whom we perceive to be very different. When you use a tool that has a similar material or quality to the area that you're clearing, often the area will respond more quickly.

L i f e

Life is the most precious and magical gift we will ever receive. Our blue planet, shining like a jewel in the depths of black space, is an orb covered with many forms of this fantastic phenomenon called life. Life-force energy is that mysterious, pulsing burst of being that we're enhancing whenever we clear the energy of homes and other places where people spend their time. Anything that enhances the quality of life, which makes its presence more keenly felt, is holy. This is what makes the art of Space Clearing such a remarkable and sacred craft.

L i g h t

Light is pure energy. Like plants, we need to absorb this energy in order to live. In traditional Feng Shui, lighting is very important because it's linked to the presence of *chi*. From the flickering warmth of a candle's flame to the brilliant fire of our sun, we're drawn to light as to a primal force. We delight in the seasons when the sun is at its zenith, and wait for its return during the hours and seasons of less light.

When you're doing your Space Clearing ceremony, you can call in the power of the light to assist you in your work. So, light candles everywhere. Throw back the curtains, and whenever possible, open the windows. Let light stream into every room, purifying and strengthening the energy there. The power of light can penetrate the thickest pools of stagnant energy, instantly dispersing them with warmth and illumination.

Love

There is no greater power on Earth than love, and when you bring this quality to your Space Clearing, true transformation will be possible. Love can turn the most difficult circumstances into scenes of health and contentment. It can warm the coldest heart and brighten the darkest depression. Space Clearing done without love is only an empty gesture that cannot be effective. Before you begin any clearing, take time to open your heart. Connect to the energy of the space you're about to clear. Focus your attention on each person who lives there, and let your heart open to them. Ask for the Creator to fill you with love and with knowledge as far as the best way to proceed. When you begin in this way, all the rest will be easy, and the result will be pure magic.

M

Mandala

Mandalas are ancient representations of wholeness. The sacred geometric symbols of which they're made have the power to generate focus and transformation within the mind. Harnessing the power of the mandala in your Space Clearing rituals will allow you to access levels of awareness that would not be possible otherwise.

The Blessing Altar can be constructed as a kind of mandala. By placing a candle in the center of the Altar Cloth and then making symmetrical arrangements of flowers and tools around it, you can form a powerful mandala that will energize everything that you do in your home. Stones, flowers, incense, crystals, leaves, and any other objects that have symbolic value for you can all be included in the creation of your Blessing Altar mandala. Each aspect of the mandala contributes to a sense of balance and unity throughout your home. The mandala you create is important, as it has the power to ground and help integrate the Space Clearing. It becomes a focal point for energy.

Medicine Wheel

The Native American version of the mandala is found in the Medicine Wheel, the great wheel of life. A Medicine Wheel will contain the Four Sacred Directions, and will be representative of all the cycles and seasons of life. Its energy encompasses birth, growth, life, death, and rebirth. It encompasses the four seasons, day and night, and the phases of the moon. The Medicine Wheel is a powerful tool for healing on both the physical and spiritual realms, and has been used in native cultures for centuries.

Ancient people understood that they were intricately linked to the cycles of the Medicine Wheel. Although modern civilization has lost that sense of connection, you can reestablish this link in your home by honoring the rhythm of nature. By invoking the spirit of nature, you can create a vital sense of health and well-being in your home. Space Clearing helps to restore a sense of balance that is very much in keeping with Native American concepts relating to wholeness and unity.

You can create your Blessing Altar in the form of a Medicine Wheel. Small stones can be placed in the shape of a circle, with four larger stones representing the four directions. Crystals or flowers can also be used instead of large stones to mark the place of the directions. The center of the circle should always contain an object that represents the Great Spirit.

Moon Time

A woman's moon time is that time of the month when her energy naturally shifts inward—during menstruation. Because the practice of Space Clearing requires an outward projection of energy, the moon time is not always a good time for a woman to perform a Space Clearing. Ancient people understood that this is when women can take time for themselves. By taking a break from their roles as nurturers and providers and by turning inward once a month, women can recharge their inner resources and have more energy for the rest of their cycle. If you're on your moon time and want to do a Space Clearing, tune in to your intuition to receive the best advice about whether to venture forward.

It's also not wise to perform a Space Clearing if you're ill or overly fatigued. Because this practice requires so much focus, clarity, and expenditure of energy, you should be feeling strong and well and relatively free of distractions when you perform a Space Clearing ceremony.

Mudras

From the Sanskrit word meaning "to heal," mudras are sacred hand gestures, sometimes called "signatures of God," which have come down to us from ancient Egypt. They've been used around the world since then—in Japan, China, Greece, Persia, and India. Mudras are particularly effective to use in Space Clearing because they have the power to seal energy. One excellent mudra you can use in your clearing is to place your hands in a prayer position over your heart. Imagine that your hands are filling up with loving energy, radiating outward from your heart chakra. Once your hands are full of this energy, you can move them away from your chest and out into the room, where they're gently dispersing this energy outward.

Music

Music is intricately bound to human emotions. A haunting melody can grip the heart and transport the mind to faraway places and long-ago times, whereas a sprightly tune can make you feel lively and light. Music can be a useful ally in generating energy in a home. Although there are times when Space Clearing is best done in silence, at other times, meditative music can actually deepen your intuitive state and assist you in your energy work. Different kinds of music will create different energies in your environment. Try out a variety of pieces to be aware of how each piece of music affects a particular environment.

Myrrh

This precious substance was one of the three gifts that the ancient wise men gave to the infant Christ child in the famous Biblical tale. Valued for its healing properties and wonderfully aromatic scent, the use of this ancient resin has continued unbroken into modern times. Both the bark and resin of the myrrh tree have been used for clearing ceremonies and for health and beauty remedies. Along with frankincense, it was rated as one of the two most popular fragrances of ancient Egypt.

N

Nature

Filling a home with the spirit of nature lends it a feeling of balance, harmony, and grace. Human beings have lived close to nature for nearly all of the 50,000 years that we've existed as a species. We have evolved in such a way as to be perfectly adapted to the natural world, so bringing elements of that world indoors makes us feel more in tune with our own basic nature, that is, the way we were before the advent of technology.

Plants, natural stones, furnishings made of wood, and other natural products all enhance a sense of well-being and connection to our environment. Using flowers, stones, water, and other natural elements in your Space Clearing rituals adds the primal power of these substances to your work. Indoor fountains and live plants throughout the home offer a continual connection to the world outdoors, which in turn leads to feelings of peace, contentment, and well-being.

Negative Energy

Negative energy can come from a variety of sources. Emotional discord, illness, or boredom can all result in a buildup of negative energy in an environment. Anything that makes you feel bad, even something as simple as an extended period of inclement weather keeping you indoors, can cause negative energy in your home. Space Clearing removes this accumulation of negativity and replaces it with a vibrant flow of revitalized energy. When you have Space Cleared a home, everything seems brighter, fresher, and more alive.

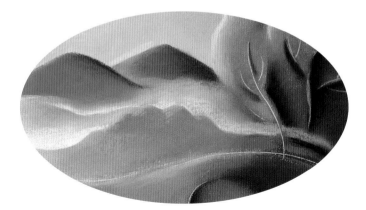

Offerings

    Offerings have always been used as a traditional part of altars and ceremonies. Throughout the world, flowers, fruit, incense, and grains have been used to represent the bounty of Mother Earth and to give thanks to her for all the gifts she gives us. What kind of offerings you make on your altar or in your Space Clearing ceremony will depend on what qualities you wish to call forth in your home. Your choice of offerings will also reflect that for which you wish to give thanks.

    Fruits represent sweetness. Grain traditionally represents abundance and the bounty of the earth. Incense carries prayers to the heavens, and flowers radiate Spirit. Offerings stay in the home after the clearing is complete and continue to ground the energy there.

O m

This ancient mantra is the sound representing ultimate reality. It is excellent for Space Clearing work. When you slowly chant this sound, allow its resonance to completely fill your being. Let your mind and body relax until you're one with the sound, the room, the Creator, and everything in the world. When you've reached this level of awareness, allow the vibration of the sound to reach out into every corner of the room. Let it penetrate the walls, the floor, the ceiling, and all of the objects therein. Know that it is attuning the energy of *all*, even as it balances and heals *you*.

P

Plants

Plants have a wonderful ability to cleanse indoor air of pollutants and toxins. In addition, they generate negative ions, which also help purify the air. To maintain a cleansed environment, it's valuable to have a few plants in your home. Ferns are particularly helpful because they generate an abundance of negative ions.

Prayer

Prayer is probably the single most valuable tool in your repertoire of Space Clearing techniques. Regardless of whether or not you consider yourself to be a religious person, prayer is a practice that takes you beyond yourself. It connects you to powerful forces that can aid you. I once knew a woman who called on the power of trees in her spiritual practice. She couldn't relate to the concept of a personal god, but she felt very connected to the majestic serenity of trees. She believed that she connected to the source of this power in her prayers. Calling for help works. Knowing you're not alone when confronted with a confusing or difficult situation strengthens your faith in your own abilities and opens your mind and heart to guidance.

When beginning your Space Clearing, take a moment to offer prayers at the Blessing Altar. You can ask for whatever help or wisdom you feel you especially need, as well as for blessings for your ceremony and for the family who lives in the space. Be sure to include words of thanks as well.

When you've completed your ceremony, return to the place where you began and offer a prayer of completion and gratitude. This seals the energy of the clearing and connects it to a source of infinite power.

Prayer Wheels

Tibetan prayer wheels are wonderful implements. They were once only used in Tibetan monasteries as a way to send blessings to the world, but they're now being used by Space Clearers. Atop an ornately decorated wooden handle rests a metal cylinder that contains thousands of hand-printed prayers. As you twirl this tool in your hand, every turn of the wheel sends prayers throughout your home. Spinning the prayer wheel as you chant is a very effective way of deepening the power of the chant. These are also excellent tools to use for blessing the land around your home.

Predecessor Energy

Predecessor energy is the energy imprint left by the people who formerly lived in a home. These energy residues can sometimes linger for years after the original owners have moved on. This phenomenon explains why it's not uncommon to discover similarities in the experiences of both the old and new occupants of a home. Even though the new owners might be completely unaware of what happened to the ones who lived there before, the predecessor energy left behind nevertheless causes the current occupants' fortunes to follow a similar path to that of the previous residents.

As a result, it's valuable to learn as much as possible about the history of a particular site. This information can guide you in choosing the most appropriate ceremonies to use in your clearing. Knowing a home's history can also influence a decision as to whether or not to purchase a piece of property. Even if you cannot determine what went on in a place you're moving into, you can still do a general clearing to remove the predecessor energy lingering there. Doing so will allow you to make a fresh start in your new home. It will also make it feel like it's completely and uniquely your own space.

Psychic Protection

When you're in a space where you truly know that you're one with all things, there's no need for psychic protection when doing Space Clearing. However, you may find at times that you may experience fears or uncertainties that would be alleviated by establishing a light shield around yourself. This sometimes happens when you're working in an unfamiliar environment, or someplace where an extremely negative series of events has taken place. In such a case, you can imagine a golden sphere of light completely enveloping you. This light shield is warm, comforting, and completely impervious to harm. All of the love and joy that is within you travels out from the light and into your environment. Love and light also comes back to you, but you're completely shielded from all negativity.

Psychic Sludge

Psychic sludge is what you feel when you walk into a room after an argument has occurred or a trauma or something unpleasant has taken place. The room may feel heavy, dark, and depressing. Sometimes taverns will contain this feeling. It's like you're walking through something dark, thick, and viscous. You may even feel a bit like taking a shower afterwards because some of the psychic sludge has attached to your auric field. Whenever you encounter psychic sludge in your home or in your aura, it's a good idea to cleanse and purify it.

Quiet

In the busy stages of preparation for a Space Clearing ritual, it's sometimes easy to forget how important it is to take time out and just be still. Silence is a great teacher. Times of quiet reflection and soulful meditation bring forth wisdom, courage, and inspiration. Go slowly. Take the time you need to fully visualize and connect to your intention. Listen to the promptings of Spirit within you. Stop. Be still. Relax. Just be.

_R_

Rattle

The rattle is an excellent tool to use in conjunction with a drum. While the drum is very well suited to breaking up heavy, stagnant energy, the rattle's talent is for smoothing, calming, and blessing the energy of an area. Rattles come in a variety of forms and sizes. They might be seeds in a dried gourd, or a leather sphere filled with small pebbles. Some rattles are traditionally created from animals' hooves tied together so that they rattle against one another when shaken. You can make your own rattles from plastic eggs that are sold at Easter. Fill them with seed beads, close them securely, and then decorate them with paper, paint, cloth, or in any way that suits your fancy. Rattles are excellent tools to use for refining energy.

Residual Energy

Whereas predecessor energy exists as a kind of energy residue that is left behind by the people who formerly *owned* a home or an object, residual energy results from the energy of the person who originally *made* the object, from its place of origin, from the materials it is made from, and from its journey since its inception.

For example, a wooden object that was carved by a craftsman in the 19th century in Germany will have a very different residual energy from something made of bamboo, crafted recently by someone living in the tropics. These things won't only *look* different, they will *feel* different in strikingly noticeable ways on an energetic level.

Residual energy isn't necessarily bad. For instance, the love that went into a sculpture during its creation may continue to radiate out of it for many years. However, it's important to be aware that all objects have residual energy. If you don't know about an object's journey, it's usually a good idea to perform a Space Clearing of its energy. As a rule of thumb, do this any time you bring something new into your home in the event that there's any stagnant residual energy connected to it. This is especially true if you purchase vintage clothing. In the Far East, many shopkeepers cleanse and bless every new item that comes into their shop to clear it of any potential negative residual energy.

Resins

The art and practice of burning resins goes back to earliest human times. Resins are derived from the sap of trees. These resins are dried to form small pellets or crystals, which are burned to release their unique scents. There is something magically evocative about the practice of burning resin incense and then wafting the smoke about a room. It calls forth images of ancient shamans chanting, of darkened churches or mosques, and of mystical ceremonies.

In order to burn resins such as frankincense or myrrh, you must first have a fireproof bowl that contains a layer of some heat-absorbing material, such as sand, soil, or salt. Then light a small charcoal briquette, holding it with a small pair of metal tongs so that you don't burn your hand. Because the tongs will also become rapidly hot, hold them with an insulating cloth or piece of leather. Be sure that no flammable objects are near you as you do this, as the charcoal can emit stray sparks when it's being lit. Once the charcoal is burning, place it in the fireproof bowl, and put small pieces of the resin on it. The resulting smoke will transform your space into a mysterious haven of ancient secrets and inner wisdom.

Aura cleansing

S

Sacred Space

Sacred Space is what you create through your practice of Space Clearing. When we're in a place that is filled with Sacred Space, we feel better. We find it easier to breathe, think, dream, and to have faith in ourselves. The space that we occupy has a profound effect upon us. Understanding this and learning how we can transform ordinary environments into Sacred Space enables us to become powerful healers of our own homes and those of others. The aim of Space Clearing is ultimately to heal the planet, one home at a time.

Sage

Traditionally used by the Plains Indians, sage has gained great popularity in recent years because of its very powerful and potent ability to cleanse and purify spaces. Its effects are instantly noticeable, and thus it is a good choice for any situation where you want to create a quick change in the feel of an environment. The pungent smell of sage smoke is very strong, so it is best for dispelling particularly heavy or stagnant energy.

Anytime you're working with burning herbs, it's very important to take care that none of the burning embers land on carpets, furnishings, or clothing. Never leave a burning bundle of herbs unattended, and use water to completely extinguish them when you're done. Many people have made the mistake of assuming a smudge bundle was out, only to come back later and find it smoldering once again.

Salt

Salt is one of the simplest, most ancient, and most common of all Space Clearing tools. That's because it has been universally recognized as a great purifier. Both sea salt and rock salt are excellent to use for clearing. Although their overall effects are the same, there are subtle differences between the two. Sea salt brings the energy of water and the ocean with it, so it's very effective for spaces dedicated to emotional healing. Rock salt comes from the earth and is more grounded in nature. It contributes to feelings of balance and integrity.

To use salt for Space Clearing, first obtain a new container of salt. Sprinkle a bit around the periphery of each room, paying particular attention to the corners, where stagnant energy tends to accumulate. Leave the salt in place for at least 24 hours before removing it so that it has enough time to fully absorb and cleanse the energy. A bit of salt can be left in the corners over time to act as an energy booster. Never eat salt that has been used in a Space Clearing ceremony. Dispose of it by putting it down a drain and running cold water until it has left the plumbing system.

Sanctuary

A sanctuary is a place of safety where you can completely relax and be yourself. A sanctuary is a home for the soul. Filling your home with things that you love—things that express who you are and what you hope to become—is a uniquely fulfilling enterprise. Space Clearing extends this concept into the realm of energy. After you've finished creating a beautiful home and a space that's truly comfortable, you'll want to balance the energy there. In this way, you will have made a place of true sanctuary for yourself and everyone who enters there.

Sealing a Room

At the completion of your Space Clearing ceremony, you will want to seal the fresh new energy that you've created throughout your home. There are several ways to do so. The simplest way is to take a moment to clearly focus on your intention for the clearing. Visualize the results that you've obtained, and mentally project a protective light around them. See this light continuing to radiate the power of the intention throughout your home in the coming days and weeks.

Another method for sealing a room or home is to draw a symbol in the air with your hand, a crystal, or with another Space Clearing tool. The sign of infinity is excellent for this purpose, but you can also choose another sign that feels right to you. This symbolically closes the clearing and sets its energy into the space.

Secondhand Furniture

Used furniture has a lot of character and charm, but it can also contain predecessor and residual energy from the previous owners. These energy traces need to be cleared in order to make the piece truly your own, and also to remove any negative energy that may have attached itself from the previous owner's experiences. Smudging a piece of furniture with sage smoke or incense is one excellent way of clearing it of residual energy. Leaving it out in the sunlight on a warm, dry day is another.

Smoke

Smoke creates a path to heaven. And blessings come down to us by the same path. Around the world and throughout the ages, smoke has been used in rituals because of this association. It is a universal connector between Heaven and Earth, between the ordinary and the Divine. Smoke purifies even as it alters consciousness. From the smoke of an open fire to the thin plume created by a stick of incense, smoke is an instant shifter of energy. It travels everywhere, and the spirit follows it on its journey.

Cleansing Your Aura with Smoke

Place a bowl of smoking herbs or incense on a table, and then draw the smoke to your body with a feather or your cupped hands. This is an excellent method to use for purifying your aura before performing a Space Clearing ceremony. As you draw the smoke over your body, focus your thoughts on your intention for the clearing. Know that the smoke is cleansing you of distractions and negativity. It is purifying your mind and body in readiness for the energy work that you are about to do.

Smudging

Bundles of dried herbs tied together with string are traditionally burned to create smoke for smudging. You can make your own herb bundles, or buy them at a New Age store or via mail order. Sage is probably the most common herb used for smudging, but other kinds work equally well. Whenever you're using burning herbs, it's very important to take special precautions not to burn yourself or to cause fires. Use an abalone shell or fireproof dish underneath the herbs to catch any stray sparks. And when you're through with your smudging ceremony, extinguish the herb bundle with water and leave it in a safe place such as a sink for a number of hours to make sure that it's truly out.

Smudging a room is an excellent method to use following an illness. Sage smoke is especially useful for this purpose. The smoke of a smudge bundle instantly creates an enormous shift in the energy of a room. It's also one of the best methods to use when you need to shift very heavy energy.

Springtime

The words *spring cleaning* bring forth images of freshly washed white curtains, of carpets being aired out in the sun, and of an overall re-creation of order and harmony in a home. These are the feelings that result from a Space Clearing as well, and springtime is the very best time to do a clearing ceremony. This is because spring is the season of new beginnings. It is the time when nature is humming with fresh and vital energy. It is the time of birth and a burst of creativity.

When you start off your spring with a Space Clearing of your environment, you can be sure that the rest of your year will go well. Get rid of what you don't need. Clean your house down to its bones. And then give it the gift of a beautiful and sacred ceremony to honor it and to call in the energy of light, healing, and harmony.

State of Mind

Your state of mind is the basis from which all your Space Clearing actions will emerge. You need to come to this process with an open heart and without any fear. Take the time you need to prepare for your ceremony. If you have doubts or fears, give them an open airing. Let them speak what they have to say so that they won't be troubling you as you work. Everyone has moments when they feel like they just can't do a clearing properly. Most of us have a nagging little voice that says, "You're going to fail at this." Listen to this voice, and then just let it fade away. There is a much more powerful reality within you that knows that you're a child of the Divine. Tune in to this reality. Let it permeate every corner of your being. Let it be the state of mind that governs your hands, your heart, your words, and all of your actions as you work to clear your home.

Stones

Stones have been used in healing and clearing ceremonies in cultures around the world. Their energy is closely aligned to that of the Earth Mother, and the grounding that they exude is highly beneficial. To deepen the energy that you wish to create in your home during your blessing and purification ceremony, you may want to create a mandala of stones on your Blessing Altar. This geometric layout of stones will ground and magnify the effect of your Space Clearing. Each stone has its own energy and characteristics, and a knowledge of these properties is very useful in choosing which ones to use for your clearing rituals. The following list will help get you started in this fascinating area:

Crystals: Crystals are very traditional tools used for Space Clearing and blessing work because they're such excellent transmitters of energy. It's best to set one quartz crystal aside that you use only for Space Clearing. It should be cleansed before you begin your ceremony, and again when you're done with it. To do this, you can rub the crystal with eucalyptus oil or wash it under cold water. Your Space Clearing crystal should be left on your tray of tools while you work. Even if you're not using it, it will hold and radiate the energy of your intention and thus empower you in your clearing. Or, you can work with a terminated crystal or crystal wand to direct the flow of energy during the clearing, or to outline sacred symbols in the air near the door to seal the room.

Stones and Gemstones for Your Blessing Altar: Stones and gemstones have been used on altars since the earliest times, and they're an excellent choice for your Blessing Altar. Each type of stone or gem elicits a particular kind of energy. Some assist healing, others can be used to promote relaxation, while others can evoke vitality. Here are some qualities commonly associated with some gems and stones:

agate	joy, success
amber	protection, healing
amethyst	spiritual attunement, compassion
aquamarine	balance, harmony
aventurine	physical healing
bloodstone	physical strengthening
carnelian	grounding
citrine	communication, mental clarity
emerald	spiritual attunement
fluorite	mental focus, calming
garnet	assertiveness, physical strength
jade	wisdom, healing
lapis	intuition, spirituality
malachite	healing, psychic power, cleansing
moonstone	emotional balancing, feminine qualities
obsidian	grounding
opal	emotional clarity

peridot	rejuvenation, mental and physical healing
quartz crystal	spiritual attunement
ruby	spiritual passion, strength
sapphire	devotion and spirituality
selenite	meditation, dreaming skills, intuition
topaz	expansion, knowledge
tourmaline	powerful purification, healing
turquoise	balancing, opening the heart

A natural stone that you gather from a special location can bring a healing energy to your Space Clearing. Additionally, a stone given to you by a teacher or someone special to you will contain the energy of that connection. Placing these stones on your Blessing Altar is one way of implanting their energy in the space.

Symbols

Symbols exert a powerful effect on the human psyche. Using symbols in your home offers a way of continually including the power of the symbol in your everyday life. You can hang a representation of a symbol that is meaningful to you on your wall, or you can purchase a sculpture of a symbol. However, there are also invisible ways of implementing the power of a symbol in your home.

If you're painting a wall, you can begin by painting the symbol on the wall with the same paint you will be using. Allow this to dry, and then paint over the entire wall. Although no one else will be able to see the symbol once you're done, it will nonetheless radiate its meaning into the room.

You can also implant symbols into the energy of a room by drawing them in the air with your hand or with a quartz crystal. You can even do this with your mind alone. Just imagine the symbol clearly in the room. See it with your mind's eye embedded in the energy field of your space, and it will continue to radiate its presence all the time.

When you're clearing your home, you can use the energy of symbols to help you achieve your intention. For example, you might choose to implant the energy of a triangle over the desk in your study, as this symbol is traditionally associated with focus and clarity. The image of a heart would be a good choice on the wall above a bed or in a child's room.

T

Tools

Like any master craftsperson's tools, those involved in your Space Clearing work will become treasured objects that you care for with love and use with pride. There is no single best tool or set of tools. You will need to experiment with many tools in order to find the ones that can work best for you. Try them out. Tune in to your intuition to discover which ones best help you project your intention and energy into a space.

Totems

A totem is a spirit animal that can offer guidance and protection to you in your Space Clearing work. One way to discover your totem animal is to go on a shamanic journey. Allow yourself to enter a state of deep meditation, and imagine that you're in a beautiful meadow. A thick fog begins to build until you can't see the meadow. Even though you can't see anything, you can feel the approach of your power animal. Reaching your hand out into the mist, touch your animal, and feel energy and strength flowing to you from your totem. As the mist clears, you can see your power animal.

Pictures or sculptures of your totem animals can be placed on your Blessing Altar or throughout your home. Doing so brings a protective energy to your Space Clearing and to your home, and also activates the qualities associated with the particular animal.

Tuning Fork

The tuning fork is a very good instrument to use when you're working with fine or delicate energy, or when you're clearing wooden objects. A tuning fork is also excellent for balancing the energy of a person when you're performing a personal clearing. Because the sounds created are so subtle, tuning forks are also especially beneficial for clearing the energy of meditation rooms and healing centers. To use a tuning fork, strike the end sharply on the heel of your hand. This will cause it to vibrate. You won't be able to hear anything, but as soon as you place the end of it on a wooden piece of furniture, you'll hear the sound as it vibrates along the wood grain.

U

Used Clothing and Jewelry

Used clothing and jewelry items carry a large charge of residual energy from the previous owners, because these items are worn in an intimate way. They are in continual contact with the body of the person wearing them; therefore, they take on huge amounts of energy from that person. When you know who owned the item before you—for example, if you receive something from a beloved relative or close friend, this can be a very positive factor. But even in these cases, there are times when you need to release the energy charge from a used possession, and it's an especially good idea to do so when you don't know who owned the item before you.

Washing clothes in detergent with a bit of lemon juice or some baking soda will clear them of residual energy. Hanging them in sunlight for a while afterwards is also an excellent idea. Passing things that cannot be washed through the smoke of a smudge bundle, or hanging them in an incense-filled room, is effective.

Sunlight is another good method to use for things that can't be washed. Jewelry can be cleansed in holy water, washed in morning dew, or left in sunlight or moonlight. Because you might not like to leave some items outdoors for long, a windowsill where sunlight or moonbeams will fall is a good choice for the cleansing of jewelry. Smudging smoke also works for clearing jewels.

Using Your Personal Power

Sometimes there is reluctance on the part of healers to fully use their power. Perhaps because power has been abused so frequently, there's a fear of crossing that line. However, when you're attuned with higher energy, the power that flows through you is a force for good. Connect to your spirit power in whatever form works best for you. Ask for guidance, for your heart to be filled with love, and for light to shine out of your heart and into the space you'll be clearing. And then don't be afraid. Go for it! Step into your power, and know that you were sent here for a purpose.

V

Visualization

Visualization is a very important aspect of Space Clearing. Ringing a bell in a room without the power of visualization behind it will only be a pleasant sound. However, when the ringing vibrations are traveling on the force of a fully visualized intention, total transformation can result! Visualization is a skill that you can practice and perfect over time. Don't worry if you aren't successful with your first efforts. And it doesn't matter if you aren't a particularly visual person, because visualization can involve all of the senses. If you're someone who is primarily kinesthetic, then imagine how you would like the room to *feel* after you're done with your clearing. Or perhaps you will imagine how the tones of a drum will *sound* after you've dispelled the negative energy. When you become skilled at visualization, what you imagine can become real.

Voice

Your voice can be a powerful tool for Space Clearing. There is power in the word, and speaking your prayers aloud can shift energy in a room. Chanting, toning, and singing can also clear a room. When using your voice for Space Clearing, clearly hold the intent for the home and its occupants while you use your voice and feel your intent traveling on the sound of your voice to every nook and cranny in the room.

Door ways as Portals

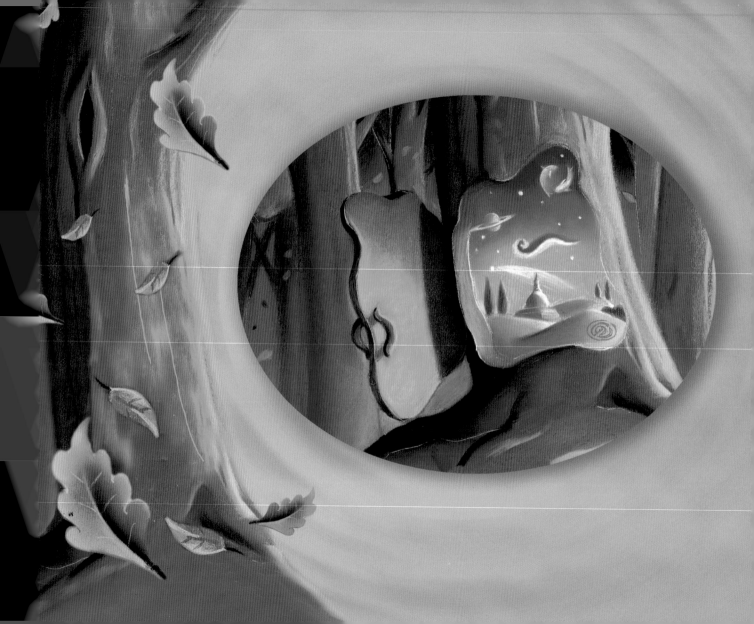

W

When to Do Space Clearing

Space Clearing will give your home a lift anytime you do it, but there are a number of instances when it's especially helpful, and there are other times when it's absolutely necessary. The following is a list of some of these times, but your own intuition is the very best guide as to when and how you should clear your home:

- Before building a new home
- Before moving into a new home
- After an unhappy event, such as an argument or an accident in the home
- After an illness, divorce, or death
- To celebrate a blessed event, such as a new baby
- To commemorate a passage, such as a graduation or marriage
- Before a party or family gathering
- Anytime you need to shift the energy of your home

Wholeness

When you've balanced the energy of a room through your Space Clearing ceremony, feelings of wholeness, peace, and integrity will result. Wholeness is a necessary ingredient for health and well-being. It is that quality present when you realize that things are no longer separate, but related to each other in an integral way. When we feel whole, we know our place in the great scheme of things, our purpose for being here, and our connection to each other and the Great Spirit.

Wind Chimes

Wind chimes are traditionally used in Feng Shui to promote the flow of *chi* through a home. In Space Clearing, they're also useful for invoking energy into the home and for preserving the intention of a ceremony. The delicate sounds created by the chimes disperse their energy throughout a home.

Windows

In Feng Shui, windows are considered to be the eyes of the home. They need to be kept clean, and should be opened frequently in order to let in light, fresh air, and fresh energy. If possible, before a substantial Space Clearing ceremony (which might be done before moving into a new home), it's an excellent idea to wash the windows, symbolically allowing light and clarity into the home. Also, during and after a Space Clearing, it's wise to open the windows to allow fresh energy into the home, weather permitting.

Y

Yin and Yang

Yin and *yang* are the two opposing yet harmonious forces in the universe. When they're in balance, then there will be harmony, beauty, health, and abundance. Space Clearing is a practice whose aims are to create the kind of harmony where everything is in balance.

Yin is inward, slow, dark, cold, and associated with the moon and the feminine spirit. Yang is outward, fast, bright, hot, and associated with the sun and the masculine spirit. In Space Clearing, if energy is too yin and feels sluggish and heavy, then use yang tools, such as loud noises made with a drum or a large clanging bell or gong. If your home feels too yang—if there are arguments occurring and the energy feels erratic and agitated—then use yin methods, such as essential oils, crystals, and soft chanting to slow and soothe the energy of your environment.

Space Clearing is the art of bringing balance and harmony to a dwelling, and when you understand the principle of yin and yang, your Space Clearing can create miracles.

❧ ❧ ❧

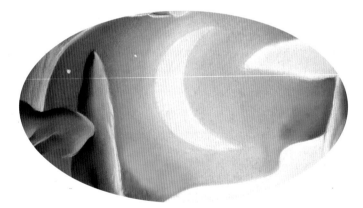

About the Author

Denise Linn has researched Space Clearing traditions from ancient and native cultures for more than 30 years, including spending time with the Maori people in New Zealand, the Aborigines in Australia, the Zulu in Africa, the kahunas in Hawaii, a shaman in Brazil—as well as exploring the traditions of Native Americans and her own Cherokee heritage. She is a renowned teacher, author, and visionary whose powerful synthesis of practical information and spirituality has had an impact on thousands of people worldwide.

Denise is the author of the groundbreaking book, *Sacred Space*, which initiated the Space Clearing movement that has gained so much recent popularity. She is also the founder of Interior Alignment,™ a professional Feng Shui certification program. Currently, Denise teaches in 19 countries and has been a featured speaker at numerous international Feng Shui conferences throughout the world.

For information about Denise Linn's professional Space Clearing and Feng Shui certification programs, contact:

INTERIOR ALIGNMENT™ PROFESSIONAL
CERTIFICATION PROGRAM
Denise Linn Seminars
P.O. Box 759
Paso Robles, CA 93447-0759
www.InteriorAlignment.com
or
www.DeniseLinn.com

Also by Denise Linn

Books

Pocketful of Dreams (1988)
Dream Lover (1990)
Past Lives, Present Dreams (1994)
Sacred Space (1995)
Signposts (1996)
Quest (1997)
Descendants (1998)—reissued as *Sacred Legacies* (1999)
Altars (1999)
Feng Shui for the Soul (1999)

Audios

Journeys into Past Lives (1999)
Life Force (1998)
Phoenix Rising (2000)

Video

Instinctive Feng Shui for Creating Sacred Space (2000)

Hay House
Lifestyles Titles

Flip Books

101 Ways to Happiness, by Louise L. Hay
101 Ways to Health and Healing, by Louise L. Hay
101 Ways to Romance, by Barbara De Angelis, Ph.D.
101 Ways to Transform Your Life, by Dr. Wayne W. Dyer

Books

A Garden of Thoughts, by Louise L. Hay
Aromatherapy A–Z, by Connie Higley, Alan Higley, and Pat Leatham

Aromatherapy 101, by Karen Downes

Colors & Numbers, by Louise L. Hay

Constant Craving A–Z, by Doreen Virtue, Ph.D.

Dream Journal, by Leon Nacson

Feng Shui Personal Paradise Cards, by Terah Kathryn Collins

Healing with Herbs and Home Remedies A–Z, by Hanna Kroeger

Healing with the Angels Oracle Cards (booklet and card pack),
by Doreen Virtue, Ph.D.

Healing with the Fairies Oracle Cards (booklet and card pack),
by Doreen Virtue, Ph.D.

Heal Your Body A–Z, by Louise L. Hay

Home Design with Feng Shui A–Z, by Terah Kathryn Collins

Homeopathy A–Z, by Dana Ullman, M.P.H.

Inner Wisdom, by Louise L. Hay

Interpreting Dreams A–Z, by Leon Nacson

A Journal of Love and Healing, by Sylvia Browne and Nancy Dufresne

Meditations, by Sylvia Browne

Natural Gardening A–Z, by Donald W. Trotter

Natural Healing for Dogs and Cats A–Z, by Cheryl Schwartz, D.V.M.

Natural Pregnancy A–Z, by Carolle Jean-Murat, M.D.

Pleasant Dreams, by Amy E. Dean

Space Clearing A–Z, by Denise Linn

Weddings A–Z, by Deborah McCoy

What Color Is Your Personality?, by Carol Ritberger, Ph.D.

What Is Spirit?, by Lexie Brockway Potamkin

You Can Heal Your Life, by Louise L. Hay

Affirmation Cards

Inner Peace Cards, by Dr. Wayne W. Dyer
Power Thought Cards, by Louise L. Hay
Wisdom Cards, by Louise L. Hay

❧ ❧ ❧

All of the above titles may be ordered by calling Hay House
at the numbers on the next page.

We hope you enjoyed
this Hay House Lifestyles book.
If you would like to receive a free catalog featuring additional
Hay House books and products, or if you would like information about
the Hay Foundation, please contact:

Hay House, Inc.
P.O. Box 5100
Carlsbad, CA 92018-5100

(760) 431-7695 or (800) 654-5126
(760) 431-6948 (fax) or (800) 650-5115 (fax)

Please visit the Hay House Website at: **hayhouse.com**